Living With the Dragon

Stepping Stones, Volume 2

William Lively

Published by William Lively, 2024.

LIVING WITH THE DRAGON

First edition. January 25, 2024.

Copyright © 2024 William Lively.

ISBN: 979-8224264933

Written by William Lively.

Also by William Lively

Stepping Stones
Stepping Stones: The Army Years, 1960-1962
Living With the Dragon

Table of Contents

Dedication

Dedicated to my wife, Nancy Jane Pye Lively who spent hours editing and making suggestions on how to improve the text.

Fortunately, for me, she kept all the letters I sent her from China during my six months there in 1995. I used these heavily to bring back memories that otherwise would have disappeared forever from my mind.

Living With the Dragon
China 1995

William O. Lively

Stepping Stones: Living With the Dragon
China 1995

We travel through life stepping from stone to stone. We always hope that we will not slip into the water, the mud or worse. There are people ahead of us and behind us as we walk through our life. Some help. Some hinder. Each decision we make is another step to a new stone. Here in these pages are some of the stones I stepped on during the summer and fall of 1995 when I was in China.

Dedication

Dedicated to my wife, Nancy Jane Pye Lively who spent hours editing and making suggestions on how to improve the text.

Fortunately, for me, she kept all the letters I sent her from China during my six months there in 1995. I used these heavily to bring back memories that otherwise would have disappeared forever from my mind.

Getting Ready

Retirement

I submitted my retirement papers in December 1994 and retired on the last day of February 1995. At that time, I had no idea I would soon be on my way to China for six months to help a friend, Qian Fupei, get ready for the First International Conference on Project Management.

Fupei had been a visiting scholar at the University of Maryland, September 1987 to September 1988. He lived with us in Annapolis during the summer of 1988 and we became good friends. Somehow he persuaded the university to invite us to visit the school. In 1989 and again in 1992 Nancy and I traveled to the campus of Northwestern Polytechnical University (NPU) in Xi'an, China. We stayed in the university guesthouse and gave a lecture to the library staff and taught English as a Second Language during the month we were there.

Letter of Invitation

Fupei knew I was to retire on the first day of March 1995. He called me at home in Annapolis in January and asked if I was interested in traveling to NPU to help him prepare for the First International Conference on Project Management. The conference was to be held at NPU, in Xi'an, China in October 1995. "I need you to go over the papers written in Chinese and put them in good English."

Perplexed I asked, "How can I do that? I cannot read Chinese characters ..."

"No, no," he broke in, "we will have the writer's department translate them. I want you to edit the translations so they will be in good English."

"Ah, ok, I can do that."

"When can you come?"

"I'll let you know," I replied.

One-time entry visa

"Good, I will have the university send you a letter of invitation. You should receive it in several weeks."

With that, I took the first step that led to many adventures and a host of memories.

Visa

A few weeks later the invitation letter arrived. I obtained a visa application. Attaching the letter to the completed application I drove to Washington, D.C. where I turned in the application and letter to the passport control office of the Chinese consulate. I was told to come back in two weeks. Following their instructions, two weeks later I returned and picked up my passport. I checked to be sure the visa was in my passport. It was there.

The visa was good for 180 days, beginning the day I entered China. I planned to leave Dulles International Airport on Sunday, April 30th, 1995, arrive in Narita, Tokyo on Monday, May 1st, and fly to Beijing on May 2nd. Thus, my visa would run for 180 days from May 2nd. This meant my visa would expire on October 29th, 1995.

Planning

Now was the time to start planning. Going away from home for six months cannot be taken lightly. Prescriptions had to be filled, clothes, snack food, and personal items bought. Travel plans had to be completed.

ATMs in China

Knowing that Nancy and I had never seen even one cash machine in 1986, 1989, or 1992, I never considered taking a credit card with me. In fact, we also had never seen an ATM. I did not want to carry cash, so travelers' checks were the answer to having Chinese currency during my six months in China. I bought twenty-five hundred dollars' worth of American Express checks. I felt I would not spend four-hundred and twenty-five dollars a month. I did not expect to come close to that figure.

Prescriptions

I could not go away for six months without my prescriptions for high blood pressure. My doctor agreed to write prescriptions allowing the pharmacist to give me six months for each medication. At first the pharmacist seemed skeptical until I explained the reason for the order. He filled the prescriptions and as he handed them to me said, "Have a good trip."

I carefully put the prescriptions in a secure pocket in my journalist jacket. Other items I could replace if necessary. Prescriptions were another matter.

Clothing

Nancy and I had learned how to travel light but being away from home for six months is quite different from being away for several weeks or a month. Fortunately, I did not have to consider winter clothing. The six months I was to be in China were warm and hot months. Keeping cool would be my problem. The trousers and shirts were not a problem. Blue jeans and khaki pants would be fine. Nancy bought me three pairs of silk underpants. These I planned to handwash each day, knowing that in the hot dry air of Xi'an they would dry overnight. My one real need was a new, fifteen pocket journalist jacket. Such a jacket would be like having a second carryon bag without it being counted as carryon. With a backpack and a journalist jacket I would not need a carryon suitcase. I knew this would make walking through airports, train stations and cities easier as my hands would be free. The trick is to memorize what goes in each pocket, i.e., airline tickets go here, writing pad goes here, passport goes here, and on and on. This avoids the frustration of searching through numerous pockets for things.

Food

I did not think food would be a problem except for when I was traveling long distances by train. I hoped and planned to make several train trips where I would be on a train for twenty-four or more hours at a time. Food I carried had to be nonperishable, not in tin cans or glass containers. It had to be packaged such that I could carry it in the big pocket on the back of my journalist jacket. Trail mix was the answer. I bought a five-pound bag of trail mix. I could separate this into zip lock bags. Thus, I would not need to worry about going hungry. Additionally, I knew that at train stops I could exit the passenger car and buy a container of Chinese instant noodles that I could cook by adding hot water from thermoses in the soft sleeper compartment. There are many choices of such noodles in China ranging from the very spicy to the bland. Spicy is best.

Help is Always Welcome

Wang Jing and Sun Hai

At that time two young people from China, who were attending St. John's College in Annapolis, Maryland, were living with us. Jing was from Hefei, the capital of Anhui Provence. Hai was from Guiyang, the capital of Guizhou Provence. We decided that I should visit both their parents.

Jing had an Aunt Lin and Uncle Kuang, living in Beijing. She contacted them asking if I could stay with them several days before I moved on to Tianjin where I would visit another friend. She also asked if her parents could host me if I was able to visit her hometown of Hefei. As it worked out all four agreed and really helped make my trip so enjoyable.

Dang Ae

My friend Dang Ae arranged for her brother, Dang He, a government official in Beijing to reserve a car and pick me up at the Beijing International Airport. He agreed to take me to where Jing's aunt and uncle lived.

Li Zhu

We met Li when she was a visiting middle school teacher living with two of our friends, Morris and Twyla Vickers. Li lived in Tianjin, about eighty miles from Beijing and said she would like me to visit and get to know her family.

<u>Matt Dillon</u>

Matt was a friend who worked several years at the same company as I. He left the company, earned a seminary degree, and was now living and taking classes at the Maritime University in Dalian. I contacted him and he asked me to please visit him, his wife and two daughters.

<u>Lu Lu</u>

Drove me to Dulles on my way to China and was always ready to help in any way possible.

<u>Others</u>

And thanks to all those I from whom I received help but have forgotten to mention. Thanks a million.

The Journey Begins

A irline tickets

Finally, everything seemed in order, and I bought roundtrip tickets on Japan Airline (JAL) from Washington Dulles International Airport to the Beijing International Airport via Tokyo Narita International Airport in Japan. The ticket included a night at the Nikko Narita hotel both going to China and returning home. I was excited and set to go on... a six-month adventure in the land of the dragon, China.

The Trip Begins

Our friends Lu Lu and Dang Ae who we had met at National Airport some years before lived in Great Falls, Virginia, near Dulles and invited us to stay with them the night before I was to fly to Japan. This saved us a long drive through traffic from Annapolis on the day of the flight. It was scheduled to take off at 1:30 p.m. Lu said he would drive me to the airport meaning that Nancy could avoid driving from Dulles back through traffic to Annapolis.

We drove to their home in Great Falls, Virginia and got up early the next day. After breakfast, Nancy left to drive home.

Dulles International Airport

Lu stopped in front of the door marked Japan Airlines. We got out together and pulled my suitcase from the trunk of the car. The suitcase was heavy. Lu started to pick up the suitcase to carry it into the terminal.

"Lu, you don't have to go in with me. It will just waste your time. I'm fine, and I know you have a lot to do today."

Lu smiled before asking, "Are you sure."?

"I'm sure," I replied. "I can manage the suitcase. It has a good handle and a good set of wheels. With my backpack and this suitcase, I can get around quite well. Thanks a bunch for bringing me to the airport. I really appreciate it very much." I was not as sure as I sounded that I could get along quite well with the suitcase.

"No problem, "Lu said, "anytime. I'm glad to do it. Have a great trip."

"I will," I replied, "I'll see you next fall."

I gave a final wave as Lu got in his car and drove away. Turning, I pulled up the handle on the suitcase, adjusted my backpack, and walked into Dulles International Airport. Surprisingly, the airport was quite empty. To my delight, since standing in line is one of my pet peeves, there was no line at the Japan Airline counter.

Walking to the counter, I handed my ticket to a young Japanese woman and placed my suitcase on the scale.

She quickly looked over my ticket and asked, "May I see your passport?"

"Of course," I replied as I unzipped a pocket on my journalist vest, withdrew my passport and handed it to her.

"Thank you," she said smiling. Deftly she opened the passport to check my picture. Flipping through the pages she also checked ensuring I had a valid visa for China.

"Do you want your bag checked through to Beijing?" She asked.

"Yes, please," I replied. "That is a heavy suitcase, and I don't want to see it again until I've arrived in Beijing." I was not looking forward to carrying a heavy suitcase through airports and train stations.

She attached the claim check to the suitcase and then handed me the receipt. "Do you need to get anything out before I send it on? You'll be staying overnight in Tokyo."

"No. But thank you, I have everything I need in my backpack for the night in Tokyo." I took the baggage claim ticket and placed it inside my passport. I put the passport back in my pocket and zipped it shut.

"Fine," she replied, "I see you have requested low-fat meals."

"Yes," I said, "and, if possible, I would like a seat beside the window at the bulkhead."

"Let me check." Quickly her fingers flew over the keyboard. "Yes, I can give you seat 35K. That is at the bulkhead." Slipping my ticket into an envelope, she penciled in my seat number. "You can go on to the gate now if you like. You have plenty of time."

"That is why I came early," I said, "I really do not like to be in a hurry."

"I wish more people came early. It would make my job easier, or at least less stressful. Thank you for flying Japan Airlines."

"Thank you," I replied as I put the ticket in another secure pocket in my vest.

I moved to the security check, placed my backpack on the moving belt of the x-ray machine, and walked through the metal detector. I had expected the machine to beep as I had a pocket full of change. However, no beep sounded. I collected my backpack and walked into the transit section of the airport.

I checked the first monitor I saw to find where I should go to catch the 'people mover.' The 'people movers' are those large, strangely shaped buses which transport passengers at Dulles from the main ticket terminal to the arrival and departure terminal.

As I had two hours before my scheduled departure, I stopped at a Starbuck's for a cup of coffee. Sitting by the glass wall, looking out over the tarmac, and taking sips of hot, strong coffee, I contemplated the adventure I was embarking upon, six months in China, the Middle Kingdom, land of the dragon. What lay ahead? I would, for the first time, be traveling alone in China. Would I be able to negotiate the Chinese train ticketing system? It is not an easy system for the independent traveler to negotiate. There are more people wanting to travel than there are tickets available. I felt some relief knowing that at each planned destination there were people, either friends or relatives of friends, waiting to put me up for the night. I am not sure how long I stood watching the activities outside the window as I contemplated. At some point, I noticed my cup was empty. Glancing at my watch, I saw I still had an hour before I needed to be at the gate. Seeing no reason to stay where I stood, I tossed the cup in a nearby trash can and made my way to the bus which would take me to the departure terminal.

Orange Man

Walking into the area where the buses come in, I saw a large group of people at the end of the terminal. As I approached the crowd, I saw a sign saying this was the boarding area for the flight to Tokyo. Looking around I spied an empty space beside a supporting column. Making my way to the column, I leaned on it and watched the crowd of waiting people. Time passed slowly, as it always does when I am waiting. As I stood watching I noticed a young Asian couple with two small children. Both were short, even by Asian standards. They were very stout, not fat. Rather, they were like fireplugs, short and strongly built. The man and his wife had a wide girth from shoulders to feet. The man wore wrinkled green shorts, a Signal Corps orange tee shirt, and well-worn sandals. His wife wore designer nylons, an extremely short frilly skirt, fancy blouse, and black high-heeled shoes. The difference in their clothing was remarkable. Their daughter sat in a stroller and their son, about four, stood tugging his mother's hand. [i]

A flight attendant approached the Orange Man. In my mind, I had tagged him with this name. I was too far away to hear the flight attendant speak. As she spoke to him, I saw a started look cross his face. Turning to his wife, he spoke rapidly and then the entire family followed the stewardess away from the loading area.

"I wonder what that is about," I wondered.

About ten minutes later, the Orange man, followed by his wife and children, returned to the loading area where an animated discussion took place. Again, I wondered what was going on between Japan Air and this couple.

Finally, an announcement sounded over the loudspeakers. The transport people movers were to begin loading. Some called these people movers mobile lounges. They were mobile, but I would never call them a lounge. There was no time to lounge around on them and they were not particularly comfortable when filled with travelers. Dulles consisted of three terminals. Large people movers took passengers from Terminal 1 to either Terminal 2 or 3 depending on where their flight was to leave. Seat assignment determined the bus I was to board. The downside of being one of the last to enter the bus was I had to stand. All seats were full. The upside was that upon arrival at the plane, I was one of the first to get off the off the bus and into the waiting area. Slowly, the doors shut, the people mover backed away from the gate. We were on our way to the plane.

Entering the plane, I made my way to my assigned seat. There was no window for me to look out of, but the large emergency door just in front of me provided plenty of leg room. Not having a window seemed like a small price to pay considering I could stretch out my legs as far as I wanted. After stowing my backpack overhead, I buckled myself into the seat and watched other passengers making their way onboard.

Soon, everyone was onboard. The Orange Man and his family were behind me taking four seats in one of the middle rows. After a few brief announcements, the usual canned speeches about seat belts and emergency doors, the plane taxied to the runway. I could hear the engines revving up, then the plane began moving down the runway, gradually gaining speed. The nose of the plane lifted, and in a few seconds the plane lifted off the runway. Next stop, Narita, Japan.

Following the great circle route, we flew across New York and Canada in a long arc, gradually turning to the west. Our northward track brought us near the Arctic Circle before we headed due west. The day was bright and clear with unlimited visibility.

A soft, feminine voice came over the intercom, "For those of you on the right side of the airplane, if you look out your window, you can see Mt. McKinley, the highest mountain in North America." Some years later the name was changed to Denali. Denali, the high or tall one, is one of several names various Indigenous people called the mountain.

I stood up and moved so I could look out a window. Mountains stretched as far as the eye could see but dominating all the peaks was Denali. "Wow," I thought, "what a rugged mountain. No wonder it is a challenge to climb." Looking down on Denali and all the surrounding mountains, I wondered if there were any mountains below which have never had a person stand on the top. It seems to me it is entirely possible. This is a remote, hard-to-reach location. People have climbed Denali only because it is the highest mountain.

Meals were served, movies were shown, drinks were offered, and lights were turned low to aid sleep. Across from the emergency door, in the center of the plane, there were four lavatories. An almost steady stream of people made their way to and from these facilities. With two small children and her own needs, I noticed Orange Man's wife making several trips to the lavatories. Apparently, taking the children to the toilet was women's work, at least on the airplane.

I motioned to a flight attendant.

"Yes," she said.

"Do you have a pen and paper I can have? I want to write a letter."

"I'll get you both," she replied. In a few minutes she returned and handed me a ballpoint pen and several sheets of rice paper. I began Letter No. 1 to Nancy. The last letter I wrote to Nancy in October was number 123.

Pee on the floor

Well into the flight, I saw Orange Man's son approach the lavatory door. He stopped and cocked his head, looking at the door. The problem of opening the door was too heavy or complex. The little boy, his back to me, made that familiar motion of unzipping his pants, and as quick as that, I heard tinkling water falling onto the carpet. Unbuckling my seatbelt, I stood to get the attention of a flight attendant. It appears Murphy, of Murphy's law, was working well this day. There was no flight attendant in sight. I looked back down the aisle to see if the boy's mother was in sight. She was nowhere to be seen. Little boys have very efficient plumbing with no interference from that demon prostate which so bedevils the older male of the species. By the time I saw there was no way to help the little boy into the toilet, there was no longer any reason to help. His need now lay in a wet circle just outside the lavatory door. Zipping his pants, he turned with a look of relief and walked back down the aisle. I assume his mother never knew what he had done. The kid was lucky his mom did not know.

Later, a flight attendant stopped. A puzzled expression came over her face. I could see her mind asking the question, "What is this?" Bending down, she patted the wet carpet. Sniffing her fingers, a knowing expression came over her face, and standing, she entered the lavatory, obviously to wash her hands of the child's gift.

I remember little of the rest of the flight to Japan other than the sun shone brightly across the Pacific. Somewhere during the flight, we passed the International Date Line and, in the wink-of-an-eye we passed into tomorrow.

We crossed the international dateline losing most of May 1st. The morning of May 1st did not exist for me.

Customs Agent

Though the flight left twenty minutes late from Dulles, we landed twenty minutes early. I was surprised when I entered Customs because almost no one was there. I had checked my suitcase through to Beijing, so I did not have to wait at the luggage carousel to pick it up. As I did not have to wait for my suitcase, I was the first to pass the initial checkpoint. I was alone as I walked to passport control. The customs agent appeared a bit surprised as I approached. I handed him my passport.

"What is your purpose in coming to Japan?"

"I am just passing through and will fly on tomorrow to China."

"Where are you staying overnight?" he wanted to know.

I was beginning to wonder why he was concerned. "At the Hotel Nikko Narita"

He looked at me, then at my passport and again at me. "Where is your luggage?"

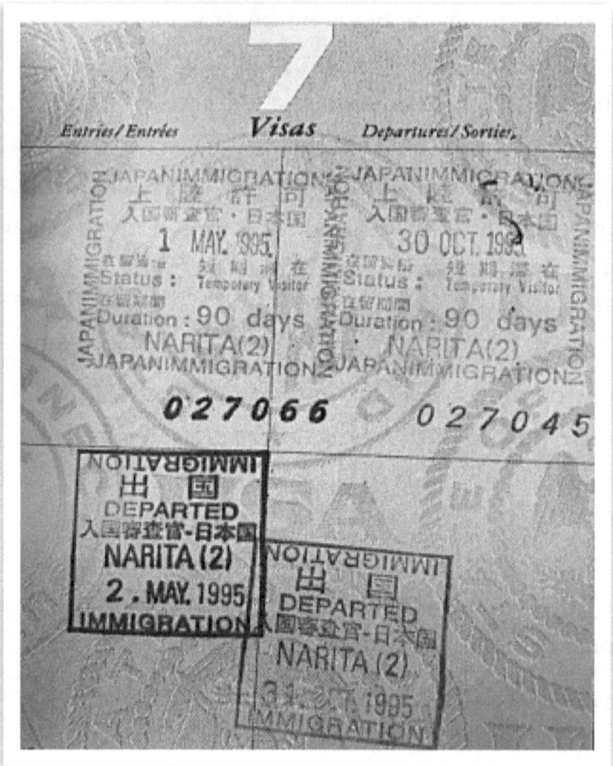

"I checked it all the way through to China," I replied. "Everything I need overnight is in my backpack."

After a long stare at my passport, he picked up a rubber stamp and, whack, stamped my passport and handed it to me. "Have a nice visit," he said.

Overnight In Japan

Hotel Nikko Narita

Rain was falling as I walked to the bus stop and waited to catch the bus to the Hotel Nikko Narita. Nancy and I had made this journey in 1989 and again in 1992 so I was familiar with the process. Standing at the stop I watched other buses arrive and leave. Finally, the Nikko Narita bus arrived, I climbed aboard. There were only three passengers. By 5:00 p.m. I was at the hotel checked into room 561. I was tired but not as exhausted as I thought I would be upon arrival.

Having eaten several meals on the plane, I had no desire for food and went directly to my room. After showering, I put on the plush, oh-so-soft white terrycloth bathrobe. Checking the channel list, I flipped on the television to the English language CNN. In a few minutes, they gave the weather forecast. I was pleased to see the forecast for Beijing the next day was partly cloudy and with the temperature in the 70s a comfortable day.

By now, I was feeling tired and decided to go to bed even though it was only a few minutes after six in the evening. Before settling in for the night, I poured a glass of hot water from the provided thermos into a glass. I thought if I woke up thirsty during the night the water would be drinkable at room temperature. Indeed, I did wake up about 1:00 a.m. thirsty and drank the water. Fortunately, I was not hungry.

Morning

No rain was falling when I got up, but it was foggy turning distant trees and building in to dimly viewed grays. To me such mornings have a beauty of their own,

Breakfast

I was up early with plenty of time to pack and be ready to leave after breakfast. The schedule for opening the restaurant doors was 6:00 a.m. I, and a man from Australia, walked up to the door five minutes early. We greeted each other good morning and those were the last and only words I was sure I understood. His pronounced Australian accent left me guessing his meaning in every sentence he spoke after that.

Breakfast was a strange mixture of Eastern and Western foods. Eggs, sausages, Miso soup, Chinese dumplings, tofu, canned corn, French fries, and many Japanese dishes I could not identify. I avoided the "strange dishes" thinking, "Why tempt my stomach before a four-hour flight to Beijing?"

Sated, I returned to my room, grabbed my backpack, and returned to the lobby to catch the 7:30 bus to the airport. I thought about buying a cup of coffee but suffered from sticker shock when I saw the price ... something like three dollars a cup. Checking in at the Japan Airline counter, the agent assigned the same seat number as yesterday, 35K. I paid the exit tax, about $25.00, passed through the passport check, and made my way to the gate where I waited to board.

Approaching Beijing International Airport

To Beijing

The flight to Beijing took off on time. Avoiding the 'strange foods' may have been an excellent idea for though the plane was a 747 for the first two hours it was a keep-your-seat-belts-fastened ride to Beijing.

The wind bounced the plane up and down and occasionally tilted the plane to the side. I sat there and thought, "What would a ride on a small 737 be like in this keep-your-seats situation?" I did not care to find out.

Several hours out of Beijing, the wind died, and the ride became smooth. The landing was a soft touchdown and slow approach to the gate where we were to exit. A flight attendant handed out customs forms an hour or so before we landed. Dutifully, I had filled them out, checking I had nothing to declare.

Exiting the airplane, I followed the crowd to the luggage carousel. There I waited for my suitcase to appear out of the bowels of the terminal. It was a long wait. As I had checked my bag through from Dulles, I believed my wait resulted from it being one of the first suitcases loaded at Narita; first on—last off. But in time, there it was, belching out of the depths onto the carousel. I had grabbed a luggage cart as I entered the room. Hauling the heavy suitcase off the carousel, I placed it on the cart and made my way to customs. The customs agent waved me through showing no interest in me, my suitcase, or my backpack. This was before 9/11 and security and customs seemed very lax. In all my travels I have encountered more delays and questions when returning home to the United States than when landing abroad.

Welcome Sight!

As I exited customs, I saw two young men and a young woman with a sign that read, "Bill Lively". What a relief. I would not have been totally lost if they had not been there. I did have the address of Jing's aunt and uncle and could have taken a taxi. However, my friend in the States, Dang Ae, told me she had contacted her brother, Dang He, who I had met in 1992. He had agreed to meet me, but he was not at the airport. I shook hands all around with the folks who he sent to meet me.

The young woman stepped forward and said, "Mr. Dang is tied up in an important meeting. He sent us to meet you and take you to your destination." One of the young men took hold of the cart and said, "Follow me. We are parked nearby."

The car was a big black Mercedes with leather upholstery. I settled in the rear seat. The young woman sat beside me. She was the spokesperson for the group. Handing me a piece of paper she said, "This is the address we were given. Is it correct?"

I compared it to the address Jing had written for me. "Yes," I said.

"That is the address I have."

"Good," she said. Then she spoke to the driver and off we went on the new limited access, four-lane highway. Built between 1992 and 1995, the road was limited access, and trees lined with shrubs planted between the trees. In 1989 and 1992 on the old road, Nancy and I saw peasants working in the fields. Walkers and bicycles also traveled on the old road. Now, in 1995 the trees and shrubbery prevented me from seeing into the fields where peasants worked. Walkers and bicycles were not allowed.

The three Chinese young people chatted with me and each other. Finally, after about an hour, we pulled into a courtyard. Jing's aunt must have been watching for she appeared before I got out of the car.

"Will you need your suitcase here?" the young woman asked.

"Actually, no, I do not. But I will have to take it with me to have in Xi'an."

Smiling, she said, "If you do not need it until you arrive in Xi'an, we will ship it there for you. Do you have an address where it should be delivered?"

I was more than surprised. I was astonished. This meant I would not have to lug this heavy suitcase all over Eastern China as I traveled and visited friends.

"Are you sure you want to do this?"

"Yes, our boss, Mr. Dang, told us to ship it if you can do without it."

"Oh, that would be wonderful" I exclaimed, "You can have it and thank you very much. I was not looking forward to lugging it around with me." I dictated the address to her and she wrote in her small notebook.

We shook hands, and I thanked them heartedly again.

By now, Jing's cousin, Helene, had joined us. In flawless English, she introduced herself.

The day had begun well and ended better than I could have hoped. Now, the adventure began in earnest.

Days in Beijing

First Day in Beijing

Morning had broken. It was 6:15 and I had been up for forty-five minutes. Here I was in Beijing, China, half a world away from home and a twelve-hour difference. It was evening in Annapolis. I tried not to make any noise as I was the only person awake and up. I did not want to disturb my hosts. The sun was shining, hanging in a high blue cloudless sky. I was surprised; a blue sky was a rare sight in Beijing. Normally, pollution obscures the sky, hills, and mountains. In 1986, and 1989, when Nancy and I were in Beijing, we had never seen a blue sky. In 1992 we woke one morning to a clear day and were surprised to see mountains nearby. Until then we had no idea the mountains were so close to the city.

I was staying with Jing Wang's aunt and uncle and their two children, Steve, and Helena. Jing, a St. John's College student, lived with us in Annapolis and walked the mile to and from school.

I stood at the open window. A soft, gentle breeze kissed my cheek as it wafted by me. I looked out into the square surrounded on four sides by apartment buildings. A small entrance led to the street. The sound of cars, trucks, and buses did not reach into the square.

I heard the clicking of high-heeled shoes but could not see the woman walking nearby. I assumed she was going to work. I heard the soft strands of Chinese music from a radio in a nearby apartment.

The only other sound was that of a man sweeping the square. A little cloud of dust rose with each swish, swish, swish of his broom. Hired sweepers make their rounds each day, sweeping up the dust and debris that have accumulated since the last sweeping.

I saw a man jogging by. To say jogging was being generous. His jogging was more of a slow walk with a short step jogging motion. But he was out, he was moving and that was exercise.

I could see a hundred or more bicycles locked to long metal racks near the apartment. Some were under a roof, protected from rain or snow. Soon these bicycles would join thousands of others as people rode off to work. It was 1995 and bicycles were still the primary mode of transportation.

This was how my first full day of a six-month stay in China began; a six-month journey that would take me many places and allow me to meet many interesting people.

Breakfast

Soon Jing's aunt came to the kitchen. "Would you like coffee?"

"Yes, that would be good," I replied. I was surprised as I had not seen coffee anywhere in China on previous trips.

We chatted and in a few minutes she sat a cup of steaming light brown liquid in front of me. I like my coffee black. This was not black, but it was my only choice. I took a sip and thought, "This tastes like a cup of cream. It is a heart attack looking for a place to happen." I could not say anything. She was giving me what she thought was a treat.

"I've never seen this type of coffee. What is it?" I was curious.

She handed me a small pack. Across the front was printed, *Nescafe Three in One Coffee.* Inside each packet were three ingredients, coffee, sugar substitute, and creamer. I said, "I have never seen this before." It was somewhat like the Maxwell House International instant coffees. I have never liked those either.

She smiled, "It is very popular in China. I use it whenever I want a cup of coffee."

Slowly I sipped the coffee. Just as I finished the cup, she put breakfast on the table. I cannot remember what she served, but it was substantial enough to hold me until lunch.

Summer Palace

Jing's aunt asked me, "Would you like to go to the Summer Palace?" I had visited the Summer Palace twice before and had enjoyed each visit."

"Yes, I would," I replied. "It is an interesting and beautiful place."

Thus, our plan for the rest of the day was set. The three of us got on a bus near the apartment. The ride was not long. We bought tickets and entered the vast complex of buildings, walkways, and a lake. There were surprisingly few visitors, nothing like I remembered from other visits.

Suzhou street

We walked to an area reconstructed to look like Suzhou, the city Chinese call the Venice of China. All the workers were dressed in period dress. Small traditionally looking buildings alongside the canal lined the street. Silk lanterns hung from the eves. Small boats rowed tourists up and down the canal. With a bit of imagination, a person could imagine they were in Suzhou several centuries ago.

I had not seen this before. This is a new area that was not open when Nancy and I visited.

End note [ii]

The Long Corridor

Later we walked down the Long Corridor. This covered walkway is almost 2,500 feet long and curves along one side of Kunming Lake. I tried to look at the hundreds of triangular paintings that are at the roof between each pair of supporting posts. The paintings on the posts and supporting beams added to the beauty of the corridor.

At the far end of the walkway is the Marble Boat. It was built in 1755. In 1893 the Empress Dowager Ciri, misused funds that were supposed to be used to build ships for the Chinese navy. Instead, she used the money to restore the marble boat. Ironically, the Marble boat does not float. It is held in place by wooden superstructure.

End note [iii]

The Marble Boat

Lin had packed a picnic lunch. We walked beside Kunming Lake and turned onto the Seventeen Arch Bridge that connects the shore to Nanhu Island where we sat and ate our lunch of a steamed bun with a hotdog type meat that had what seemed like a plastic casing that when bitten gave of a loud pop.

Bei Da University

We left the Summer Palace and rode a crowded bus to tour the Bei Da University campus. The guard at the entrance made me register. For some reason, he did not think I was Chinese. We found this amusing. I showed him my passport and signed the guest register so I could go on the campus.

On the campus was a white marble statue of Edgar Snow[iv] with the carved, golden painted words, *A Friend to the Chinese People*. I also saw the Arthur Sackler Museum of Art and Architecture, but we did not enter. It has a large architecturally traditional Chinese design.

Bei Da had torn down one of the walls that surrounded the campus and replaced it with stores, office space, and restaurants. The project had just been completed.

Leaving the campus, we stopped at a post office where I bought twenty envelopes and stamps. It had been a good busy day that ended with a good meal of noodles with vegetables and small pieces of pork.

Second Day in Beijing

I was up early. Breakfast consisted of steamed buns filled with red bean paste and coffee, the three-in-one that I had yesterday.

When I arrived in Beijing, I had no time to exchange money. Whether at home or in a foreign country a person needs some cash. The barter system went out long ago.

Pirated Software and DVDs

After breakfast, Jing's aunt told her son, Steve, to take me to the bank to exchange money. We walked several blocks and entered the Bank of China. We had passed a block filled with men selling pirated software and movies.

I looked at about thirty software programs, all for sale, including Word Perfect, several Microsoft programs, several Borland programs, and others. The asking price was ¥40 or about $5.00. Steve said the quality control is bad and you buy at your own risk. Some will work and some will not.

Intellectual property rights were a totally foreign concept in the Chinese culture. It is possible that they want to guard their own intellectual property, but the right of a foreigner or a foreign company to honor their intellectual property is just not a rational idea to the Chinese. Some years later, while in China, I was told by a man living in Canada whose company deals with China, "When a contract is signed, the Chinese insist that you live by the letter, by every jot-and-tittle of the contract. But for them, the signed contract and all its clauses are simply negotiating points.

Changing Money in Beijing

The basic unit of currency in China is the Renmenbi (RMB)/ RMB means the people's money. The unit of money most often discussed is the Yuan which is like the dollar further broken down in units of 10s. Though in Chinese is it is officially called the Yuan, it is called a kwai when people speak about money.[v] This can be confusing when you have three bills with Yuan written on them and the price of an item is said to be three kwai.

We joined the short line at the exchange window. There were only two people ahead of me. One man was dressed in a People's Liberation Army (PLA) uniform. The second was in a business suit. We waited for five minutes. During this time, no bank clerk appeared on the other side of the counter. Finally, a bank employee walked up and slid an aluminum briefcase under the bars of the counter.

Quickly, the man in the military uniform slid the briefcase forward, unsnapped the locks, and raised the lid just a few inches. The case was filled with wrapped bundles of money.

"Wow," I thought, "that is a lot of money. I bet it is payday at one of the military posts here in Beijing." I decided this was not the time to appear as if I were too interested in what they had in the suitcase, so I tried to appear as uninterested as possible. Satisfied, the man snapped the briefcase shut and walked away.

I exchanged a traveler's check, $50.00 into RMB. That amount of money would go a long way in 1995.

Steve said, "This is the first time I have ever been in a bank. I am not impressed with the speed of their service."

When we got back home, Helena, the daughter in the family, came to the kitchen. We had agreed the night before that she and I would go to a nearby park where a minority group fair was being held. China recognizes 56 minority groups. I do not know how many unofficial minority groups there are in China.

University Class

Helena had received permission from one of her professors for me to attend a two-hour English class with her. The first hour was devoted to reviewing the mid-term examination. The second hour was a regular instruction class. Her teacher had studied at the University of Edinberg in Scotland. She had a beautiful Scottish accent. I found the class interesting. However, it was obvious that many of the students were bored and gave lackluster responses to questions.

After class, we walked around the campus stopping at her dorm. Several of her friends had joined us. As we approached the dorm Helena said, "You can't go in just now. Wait for us."

I waited and several minutes went by. Helena came out, "You can come in now. We had to tidy up the room. It was a mess". The room was cramped with beds leaving little room for personal items or books.

It was time for lunch and we three went to the 'restaurant area' of the campus. Prices were inexpensive and I bought lunch for everyone, noodles, fried rice, sweet and sour pork, chicken with peanuts and cucumbers, and a vegetable. We could not eat it all and one of Helena's friends boxed up the leftovers. The leftovers would be her supper.

The university was near the Friendship Hotel where Nancy and I had stayed on an earlier trip to China. Helena and I walked to the hotel bookstore where I found a three-volume boxed set of *The Three Kingdoms*, one of the Chinese classics.

The ride back to her home was uncomfortable as the temperature was in the eighties and the bus was hot. Helena had a four o'clock class that she returned to attend. I began reading *The Three Kingdoms* before taking a long nap.

Free Market

Lin, Steve, Helena, and I took a long walk to the outdoor free market in their area of Beijing. The free markets are like farmers' markets in the States with many stalls selling a variety of goods. I was interested in the beautiful watermelons, pineapples, strawberries, oranges, bananas, and pears that were in abundance.

Helena said, "I love ice cream. Let's buy some."

"Do you like banana splits?" I asked.

She frowned, "I have never heard of them. What are they?"

I explained how banana splits are made and her eyes lit up. "That sounds like a dish from heaven," she said.

I should have bought several bananas and some ice cream but didn't. We walked along, looking at all the goods for sale.

Minority Fair

We left the apartment about 9:30 and walked to the Bamboo Park. It was not a long walk. Sections of the park had been assigned to different groups each dressed in their native costume. Women wore elaborate head dresses and colorful costumes. Many had fires going preparing food. One group jumped out at me. Each person, man, woman, and child had the short, stocky, muscular look of the Orange Man and his family. Sadly, I was not smart enough to snap a photo. Another group had planted a large pole in the ground. Set at step intervals were butcher knives, sharp side up. As Helena and I stood watching a man walked up to the poll. Before climbing he went through a series of hand movements and intertwining of his fingers. Then he carefully climbed grasping a knife in his hand and carefully stepping with bare feet on the knives as he climbed the poll. Just as carefully he descended to the ground. I did not want to think about what might have happened if his foot or hand slipped.

Stepping carefully

Helena and I walked around the park for an hour or more. As we left the park Helena asked me if I would like to see the National Library, China's Library of Congress.

"Sure," I replied. "That should be interesting."

"Because it is Saturday the library is closed. We won't be able to go inside. We can look from outside the fence."

We left the park and turned left on a wide street. It was a short walk to the library. Walking around the building we viewed it from several sides. To me the architecture was modern, glass and steel and not interesting.

Beijing Zoo

Then we walked to the Beijing Zoo looking at birds, the big cats, and snakes. We stayed for an hour or two before returning to the apartment. When we arrived, we sat down and had a meal of Peking Duck.

American Chicken & Ice Cream

The very popular KFC has brought the idea of 'American chicken' to China. I saw several shops selling rotisserie chicken as well as several KFCs as we traveled around Beijing. Also, I saw ice cream for sale from American companies, Carvel and Meadow Gold. This is quite a change from my first visit to China. The only American product I saw for sale in 1986 was Coca Cola.

Li Zhi Calls

Late in the day Li called saying she would come to Beijing the next day. She hoped to arrive about 11:00. I would travel with her to Tianjin and spend several days there before going on to visit Matt in Dalian.

Tianjin

Li Zhi Arrives

Li arrived at 9:30 a.m., earlier than we expected. One of her friends, the head of a work unit, asked one of his drivers to use the work unit car and drive to Beijing to take me to Tianjin with Li. The seventy-mile drive took about an hour. I was told it is a two-hour trip by train. The highway between the two cities is like an interstate highway, limited access and two lanes each direction. The land is as flat as the proverbial pancake with the road running straight as an arrow. Traffic was light.

Tianjin was designated as a special economic zone. We passed the city limit sign and drove for at least thirty minutes before entering the city proper.

Tianjin Normal University

Li and her husband lived in a small one room apartment just off the campus of the Tianjin Normal University. The apartment was far too small for me to stay with them. Li's husband, Han, teaches at the university and made reservations for me to stay in their guesthouse. He also worked with an import-export company. It was an easy walk from there to their apartment. The Tianjin TV tower looms just off the campus. It is a beautiful structure, especially at night when colorful lights play over the tower.

We ate our evening meal at Li's mother's. She lived in a building a few steps from Li and Han's home. After eating I returned to the guesthouse.

My room was on the second floor. I was surprised to learn this is the floor for Chinese guests. Thus, I had to use the stairway for Chinese guests. I could not use the stairway for foreign guests. The doors on the foreigner's stairway were kept locked.

There was no tub in my bathroom. The water from the shower ran across the floor to a drain. There was no lip on the shower as the drain was not within the shower. There were two beds in my room. One was very hard, the second was simply hard. There was a small table and chair, and a coat rack but no closet. I did have a TV. Linoleum covered the floor and there was an air conditioner in the window. The newspaper that was wrapped around the AC for the winter was still in place. The night air was deliciously cool when I opened the window. There were no pictures on the wall. A deadbolt secured the door, and a fluorescent light brightened the room.

There were foreign students here and one foreign teacher. The students lived on the first floor. I overheard four foreign students talking, one was

American and three were Brits. Li's husband said there are several Korean students. I never saw any Koreans.

Culture Street

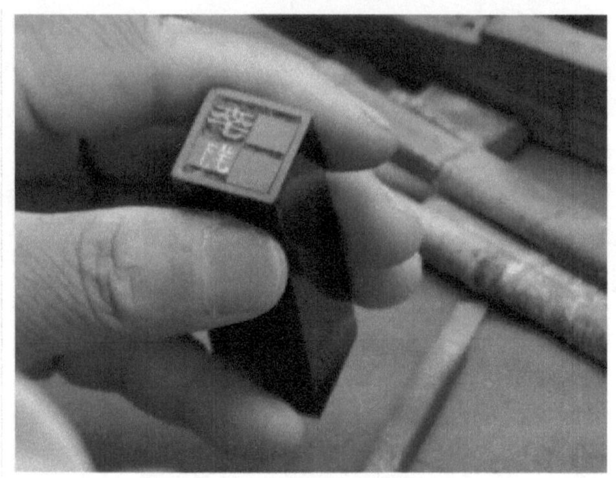

Chop being carved

One morning we went to Culture Street where all the buildings look like ancient China. This was done to attract tourists. There were a huge variety of items for sale, everything from inexpensive trinkets to extremely expensive pottery, paintings, and needlework.

Many tourists bought Chinese chops which were popular. Made from stone the chop can be used like a rubber stamp. In ancient China a document was not a legal document unless it had the stamp of one or more chops.

We then toured a thousand-year-old Daoist Temple that was on Culture Street. Though there were people burning incense and praying it seemed to me the primary emphasis was to sell trinkets to tourists.

Taxis

Nancy and I spent a month in Xi'an in 1992. A change I noticed was that the number of taxis had grown. They were everywhere, there were hundreds of them and all of them looked alike. To me they looked like yellow bread boxes, small, rectangular like a loaf of bread. Riders entered through a sliding side door.

One afternoon Li and I rode a taxi from downtown to outside her apartment. As the driver drove around a rotary I happened to look back and saw a traffic policeman pointing at our taxi and making a motion for our driver to stop. I do not believe the driver saw the policeman's signal as he kept driving. The traffic cop took a pad and pencil out of his pocket and began writing. I believe he was noting the license number of the car. I have often wondered what kind of trouble the driver experienced for not stopping.

I developed a healthy hatred of the continuous blaring horns of taxis as they prowled the streets.

43rd World Table Tennis Tournament

The 43rd World Table Tennis tournament was in progress in Tianjin when I arrived. The city government had gone all out to beautify the city emphasizing the rose, the city flower. The tree-lined streets were full of rose bushes, all in full bloom.

Li said, "My middle school is going to the tournament, and I have a ticket for you. It is a short walk from the Normal University, and we can meet there tomorrow." She told me what door the students would enter and gave me my ticket.

I met Li and the students at the appointed time. My ticket put me in a good location. I was near one of the ping-pong tables. The gymnasium was full. I saw no empty seats. Multiple ping-pong tables filled the gym. The matches were continuous. As soon as one game or match ended another began.

During the day I was amazed at how good, even the 'bad' players were. The speed of the ball going back and forth was astounding. In the end China won every category in the tournament.

Breakfast at McDonald's

The next morning, I stepped out of the guest house of the Tianjin Normal College into the cool morning air. The golden sun was rising over the sports field. It was May, too early to be concerned about the heat of summer and too late to worry about the cold of winter. Making my way across the campus, I turned left onto a footpath that took me past a sports field and ended on a short narrow street. Li Zhi and her husband's nearby apartment was on this street. But first I had to have breakfast. Other universities I visited later had street food vendors where a person could buy breakfast, i.e., mantou, large, steamed buns sometimes filled with bean paste but more often just steamed bread. There was deep fried bread, which to me were heart attacks looking for a place to happen. I could squeeze this bread and grease would drip off my hand. There was congee, a flour paste tasting gruel made of overly boiled rice and water. There were little round breads rather like English muffins. Alas, there was no such morning market at the Tianjin Teacher's College.

At other universities street vendors were easy to see. If you could not see them, you could tell by the direction people walked carrying cups, pots, pans, or bags. Some were buying breakfast for themselves, others for the entire family. Street food was inexpensive and filling. If the vendors were in sight, I could see the smoke and steam rising from the woks and griddles. Some woks were filled with grease for deep fat frying. Some were filled with water and rice from which congee, that flour paste tasting soup was made. There often was steamed bread,

Mantou, steamed buns

deep fried bread, and other foods.

From the college, I walked along the short street to a major one where I turned right. The sun cast a warm golden glow as I walked along. Roses bloomed along the street the entire distance to McDonald's, about a mile. Near the restaurant was a large digital bulletin board, the first I had seen. Advertisements rotated on the large display. Morning traffic flowed in both directions.

Finally, I arrived at the intersection. Crossing the street, I entered McDonald's, and placed my order, a hamburger, fries, and a soft drink. In 1995 McDonald's did not serve breakfast items, such as Egg McMuffin's, hash browns, sausage, or other breakfast foods. My choice was a hamburger or a big Mac. If I was really hungry, I could add French fries. There was a small extra charge for a packet of catsup.

As I ate, I watched a man mopping the floor. He was always mopping the floor or washing the windows. As soon as he finished one job, he began the next. Washing, mopping, washing, mopping continuously. It was the cleanest McDonald's I had ever seen.

After eating breakfast, I retraced my steps in time to meet Li Zhi and her son. She said the law in China was that any child below third grade had to be accompanied to school by an adult. We walked past the McDonald's turned left and walked another quarter to half a mile to Han Biao's school. There he kissed his mom and ran into the building.

Old American Husband

Turning to me Li Zhi said, "I want to take you downtown today. I am free until late today and I want you to see that area. I need to go to a bank and a department store. I think you will find it interesting."

"That's fine with me," I said. "Let's go."

Walking along a tree-lined street we stopped at the first bus stop. There were many buses running during the morning rush hour, with thousands of people heading off to work. Standing with the crowd, we shoved our way onto the third bus that stopped before us. Off we went on a twenty-minute ride. Exiting the bus, I looked around. Large trees lined this street. The architecture of the buildings spoke of Europe in the 1920's or 1930's. "This could be a set for a city movie back in the 1930's," I said.

Li Zhi smiled. "Yes, it has a European or American look. Those were heady days for foreigners." Pointing across the street Li continued. "I need to go to the bank."

We entered the building. The atmosphere of the large bank reminded me of banks when I was a kid. The ceiling was high, giving me a feeling of being in a cathedral. The floor was highly polished stone. The counter was marble with iron rods separating the bank tellers from customers. Li conducted her business. Turning to me, she said, "I want to take you to a large department store. Also, I want to look at blouses."

Shopping is one of my least favorite activities, but I was with Li, and this was her trip downtown. We walked out of the bank, turned right on the sidewalk, and made our way along the street. After several blocks and a number of turns, we entered a large department store. The lady's clothing department was on one of the upper floors, the 7th or 8th. Li began looking at blouses, and I just looked around. There was little to distinguish the department from that in large American clothing departments. Twenty or so minutes later, Li had selected two blouses, paid for them, and put them in a shopping bag. While Li had looked at blouses and I had looked at various displays, I noticed I received long stares from other women customers and store clerks. I was sure I knew why.

Later in the day as Li and I talked she said, "Did you notice how the clerks and women shoppers stared at you today?"

"Yes," I replied. "And I am sure I know what they were thinking."

Smiling, Li asked, "What were they thinking?"

"They were thinking, 'ah, she went to America and married that rich old American.' Now they are visiting and spending money."

Laughing Li exclaimed, "That's right. That is exactly what they were thinking."

Well," I said laughing, "we gave them something to talk about at work and at home tonight."

My time in Tianjin was coming to an end. My next stop was to visit my friend Matt in Dalian on the Liodong Peninsula. Li and her husband said the best way to travel was by an overnight ferry from Hangu, the seaport east of Tianjin, to Dalian. I was relieved when they said, "We will go with you tomorrow to buy a third-class ticket." That was fine with me. I needed all the help I could get.

Tianjin to Dalian

Bus to Hangu

The room was dark, bare, and dank. Concrete floors, walls, ceilings, all were covered by a faded, flaking, blue paint. An unlit single bare bulb hung from the ceiling. Light entered through the open door and filtered through two dirty windows. The ticket agent sat behind a window which was not a window, but a six by nine-inch hole cut through the concrete wall at the far end of the room. Li Zhi joined the queue. Gradually, the people ahead of her completed their purchase of a ticket, turned, and left the building. Finally, Li Zhi stood at the head of the line. I watched as she negotiated and bought a third-class ticket on the overnight ship from Tianjin's port to Dalian, a trip of just over two-hundred miles across the Bohai Sea.

Li Zhi handed me the ticket. "Now you're all set to go," she said. "There is a bus outside that will take you to the port of Hangu."

I stored the ticket safely in a zipper pocket of my photographer's vest. "How long will the bus ride be to Hangu?" I had never heard of this port.

She pursed her lips, "I guess, about an hour. I can't remember exactly."

"More like two hours," Han, Li Zhi's husband, said smiling. "I go there often to supervise the packing of cargo containers. We export our containers through Hangu."

I felt apprehensive as I was about to set off traveling alone for the first-time inside China. In my earlier travels, I had always traveled with at least one other person. Here I was the only "foreign devil" in a sea of Chinese. I was not a citizen of the Middle Kingdom. I was a *wàiguórén*, an outside the wall person.

Han, stood beside me. "Just follow people from the bus when you get to the dock. They will know where they are going."

Laughing nervously, I replied, "And if they don't know at least they can read the signs."

"That's right," Han laughed, "but you will be all right. You should have no problem. If you have problems just ask, someone on the bus will speak English."

Together, we walked into the bright sunlight and crossed the street. "Go ahead, get on now so you can have a window seat," Han said.

I sighted the sun as I climbed on the bus and sat on the shady side. I had no illusion the bus would be air-conditioned. I did not want to sit for two hours with the late May sun roasting me. Han and Li Zhi came aboard for a last few minutes of conversation. With a final goodbye they left the bus and walked away.

"Well, Bill," I thought, "don't panic now." I unzipped a pocket on my journalist vest, checked the ticket, slipped it back into the pocket and zipped it securely shut. There was no overhead rack, so I stuffed my backpack between my legs and the seat in front of me.

"Thank God I don't have a suitcase with me," I thought. Reaching forward I slid the window open. The fresh air felt pleasant against my face. The bus was filling rapidly with fellow travelers. There were no empty seats by the time we left.

Surprisingly no one spoke or asked if they could practice their English with me. Everyone busily settled down for the trip as they chatted with friends or family members. Packages, bundles, and brightly striped plastic bags were jammed, and stuffed in every available empty spot. Leftover bags sat on people's laps. As soon as they sat down most of the men lit cigarettes and the women began eating dried watermelon seeds and spitting them on the floor.

A thin little driver climbed into the seat. Placing the key in the ignition he hit the starter button. The engine coughed and hacked like a smoker just waking in the morning but did not start. He tried to start the engine again, with the same result. Again, and again the driver turned the key in the ignition. I lost count of the number of times he hit the starter button. Finally, the engine coughed to life. There was a great grinding of gears, and the bus slowly began moving forward.

"Precious Jesus," I thought, "I'm don't believe this bus will make it to the first intersection much less to the port of Hangu. This is a very tired bus." The outside of the bus was rusty with paint peeling from the metal. I hoped the engine was in better shape than the bus body. "Oh, foolish person," I thought.

Gradually the bus picked up speed. Fortunately, we hit three green lights in a row. As we passed the second light, the bus felt as if it had reached a speed of at least fifteen miles per hour. As luck would have it our fourth stoplight was red. My level of apprehension shot up. When the light turned green there was the grinding of gears and the gradual movement and pick up of speed. We approached an intersection where the road we were on crossed over the intersecting road by a bridge. We started up the incline. The bus slowed dramatically and continued to lose speed. Just as I was sure the bus was grinding to a halt, the road leveled, and the speed gradually increased. "I hope that's the steepest 'hill' we have on this trip," I thought. Fortunately, it was the only 'hill.' The rest of the trip was through country that would make the flat land of Iowa look hilly.

Now my concern was not finding the ship when we arrived. My concern continued to be would we arrive at the port on time? Would we arrive at the port today? Would we ever arrive at the port? If I were a betting man, I would have given odds that we would not make the port. I decided that I'm not a betting man, but I must be a gambling man. Here I sat gambling that this bus would succeed in arriving, not just today, but in time to catch the ship to Dalian! This was now an exercise of blind faith.

Slowly we rolled through the city. Every stop I feared would be the "last stop," that the bus, with a clash and a clank, would breathe its last and die. Happily, that day, whatever god looks over busses decided not to "call this one home to the junkyard in the sky." At every stop there was a gnashing of the clutch and gears, but with a growing reluctant effort the bus gradually inched its way forward toward our destination.

Along the way the driver pulled to the side of the road several times stopping to allow passengers on or off the bus. At each stop I sent a prayer heavenward. My fellow travelers seemed unconcerned. They either had great "blind" faith or were resigned to accepting whatever fate lay ahead, for us and the bus.

About an hour out of Tianjin the driver turned to the right, off the highway and onto a narrow road. "We must be getting close," I thought. I looked ahead and to my horror saw a line of stopped traffic. A long line of vehicles disappeared in the distance ahead of us. "And I thought we were so close," I groaned to myself. "No traffic coming toward us," I thought, "I guess there is an accident ahead blocking both lanes. The gods must be laughing at this little joke. They allowed the bus to live on but blocked the road. What a great joke."

The driver brought the bus to a grinding stop behind a tractor-trailer truck. To our right another small road disappeared into the distance. Suddenly the driver brought the bus to life again. Slowly and carefully, he backed the bus. Backing and going forward he gradually turned the bus until we were driving back the way we had come. Arriving back at the highway he turned right; in the direction we had previously traveled. "Well," I thought, "either he knows another way to the ship terminal, or he has decided to skip that stop today. Whatever, I'm onboard and along for the ride, wherever the ride is going." I noticed that no one seemed upset. Assuming this was a good sign I watched the flat countryside pass-by.

Welcome Help

We traveled another fifteen minutes and the driver turned onto a small road leading away from the highway. By now the land was sandy with scrubby plants growing at random. After another ten minutes the bus turned into a large parking area. I looked around but saw no terminal, no cranes, and no ships. As the bus stopped people stood up and began gathering their boxes, and belongings together. I suppose I looked like a little lost puppy. A young woman in a bright red dress turned to me and said, "We've arrived. This is where we get off. Follow me. We are to get on another bus which will take us to the ship."

"Thank you!" I exclaimed. "I appreciate your telling me."

Picking up my backpack, I got off the bus and joined the crowd beside the terminal bus. Suddenly the doors on the terminal bus opened. The mob surged forward, pushing, shoving, and elbowing their way aboard. There were no orderly lines here. Waiting in line appears not to be a part of the Chinese culture.

I quickly surveyed the situation and determined my strategy. Standing at the edge of the crowd I moved forward as the bus filled. Just as I felt the doors were about to close, I pressed against the man immediately in front of me. Like a halfback, allowing him, my lineman, to be my interference, I followed him onto the bus. He pushed and shoved. I followed and stepped onto the bus as the doors closed. Giving an extra shove I managed to get my body and my backpack inside.[vi] Looking around I saw the woman in the red dress looking my way. Seeing I had made it aboard she flashed a big smile. Packed butt to belly and belly to butt there was not enough room to give a thumbs up.

With a jolt the bus set into motion across the parking area, around a construction site, along long rows of shipping containers and trucks. Between the sun and the press of bodies the temperature inside the bus rose rapidly. "I hope my deodorant holds," I thought as we bounced along.

Soon the bus stopped, and the doors slid open. Being at the door I was the first one out. I stood to one side as I had no idea what to do next. I stood there for a few seconds and then followed the red-dressed lady and other travelers toward a large gray building. Passing through a large set of double doors I was confronted by a long set of stairs. "Precious Lord," I mused, "I'm so glad my suitcase is being sent to Xi'an by train. What a hassle this would be if I were lugging my suitcase behind me."

The Waiting Room

At the top of the stairway, I followed the crowd into a large waiting room, which was at least a hundred feet long and thirty feet deep. Padded benches ran the length of the room. Earlier arrivals lay asleep using their bundles as pillows. I walked forward and chose a seat near a large set of doors. I hoped the doors were the exit through which we would pass on our way to the ship.

I looked at my watch, 12:30. The schedule listed 2:30 as boarding time and 3:00 as the time we were to set sail. "Hmmmm, I thought. I have awhile to wait. I think I'll read a book." Pulling a *Brother Cadfeld* book from my backpack I settled down and began reading. Gradually the room filled as more travelers entered the room. I realized that other buses must be arriving disgorging passengers who joined us in our wait. I nodded to a man who had just sat beside me.

A New Helpful Friend

"Hello," he said,

"You speak English," I said. Perhaps it was not a bright response.

"Just a little," he responded. "Where are you from?"

"I'm from the United States," I said. "I've been visiting a friend in Tianjin."

"Ah," he said shaking his head. "Did you enjoy your visit?"

"Yes, I did, very much. Tianjin is an interesting city. Do you live in Tianjin?" I asked.

Shaking his head, "No. I live in Dalian. I came to Tianjin to attend the World Table Tennis Championships. Did you know about them?"

"Yes," I replied, "I was able to attend one day. The Chinese did very well."

Smiling proudly, he replied, "Yes they did. I played on the team years ago. I visited my old coach. I'm happy for him, for the team."

We continued our conversation. "Follow me," he said, "I will give you my room number and show you to your room. If you need anything come, see me."

"I appreciate that very much," I replied. "I think I will be all right."

"Yes," he cut in, "but remember, if you need anything see me. Also, let me give you my card. If you need anything while you are in Dalian call me."

"I will." I replied. "I'm going to Dalian to visit friends. I have an American friend who is studying Chinese at the Maritime University."

"Oh!" he said in surprise, "That is close to my university. It will be easy to find me if you need to."

Onto the Ship

I took his card and put it in a safe pocket. We continued talking as we waited until a whistle blew. "Follow me, it is time to board the ship," my new friend said.

I put my backpack on and followed him through the double doors. Two young men checked my ticket and waved me through the gate. Down a set of stairs, across the dock and up a loading ramp I followed, like a baby duckling following its mother. Turning he said, "I'll show you your room."

"Great," I said, "thank you very much."

We walked up two flights of stairs and turned toward the aft part of the ship. Stopping just in front of an open door leading to the deck he turned, "Here is your room. Your bunk is the top one on the right side. Remember if you need anything, let me know."

Shaking his hand, I thanked him. I appreciated his help. He turned and walked back down the hallway. I entered and looked around the tiny room. A metal tag with the number 145 was glued to my bunk. Four double bunk beds lined each wall. The springs looked like medieval woven chain mail. A thin mattress covered the springs. A pillow and a folded blanket lay on top of the mattress. I stowed my backpack on top of a metal locker beside the door near my pillow. Soon five men and an elderly woman joined me in the cabin. They nodded to me and promptly ignored me and began to stow their belongings. I felt some relief by their ignoring me. My Chinese was poor, and their English was nonexistent.

I was emotionally exhausted by my concern on the bus ride. Feeling exhausted I lay down to rest and at once fell asleep. When I awoke the ship was moving, only blue water was visible through the porthole. I was a bit disappointed as I had expected to watch the ship cast off and pull away from the pier.

Three men sat by the open porthole talking. A refreshing breeze blew through the cabin. Promptly I fell asleep again and though I had already slept several hours; I slept soundly until early the next morning.

Waking Up

I woke feeling as if I were suffocating. The temperature in the room had to be close to a hundred. Sometime during the night one of my fellow cabinmates closed both the door and the window. Seven bodies confined in a small space is like a flock of sick chickens in a closed coop. The temperature and humidity steadily rose through the night. My first thought upon waking was, "Oh well, I'll just go back to sleep." My second thought tumbling into my consciousness screaming, "I can't stand it in here! God, I've got to get outside to fresh air before I suffocate!" The air in the room felt and smelled sick. It felt as the air had the ability to carry every contagious disease known to man and probably several unknown diseases.

I slipped out of my top bunk, dropped to the floor as quietly as I could and put on my clothes. Grabbing my backpack, I left the room ... never to return. The cold predawn morning air, filled with the smell of the sea, washed over me as I stepped out onto the dark deck. Relief is far too tame a word to describe the wondrous feeling of that cold, clear, crisp air. I felt as if I'd been saved from the depths of a hot, airless, disease-ridden hole. I wondered, "How could they stand to continue sleeping in the sick, fetid air of the room?" Cold though it was on deck, I was not going back to the cabin for any reason. I found a spot that protected me from the cold sea breeze that swept over the deck. I realized that by water several hundred miles to my right lay North Korea. I had no desire to go there.

Out on deck

The sky in the East began to turn pink, then violet gradually turning to red. Kipling said, "An' the dawn comes up like thunder outer China 'crost the Bay."[vii] Perhaps dawn is like thunder in India, but on the Bohai Sea dawn came up glorious on a clear day. A light haze filled the air. Occasionally I saw small fishing boats heading out to sea. Seeing fisherman so far out so early in the morning amazed me. Five hours, by ship, from Dalian seemed a long way to venture forth for fish. But a man must make a living for himself and his family.

Alone, a rare occurrence in China, on the deck of a ship crossing the Bohai Sea I contemplated all that had occurred which brought me to this moment in time. The chance meeting of Chinese scholars visiting the United States for a year. Our hosting a number of these scholars in our home and taking them along on our summer vacations. Having Chinese college students living in our home. Meeting Li Zhi when she was an exchange middle school teacher in the States. The invitation to live in China and help the Management Department of the Northwestern Polytechnical University prepare for the First International Project Management Conference to be held in China. So many seemingly chance happenings all coming together and bringing me to this cold deck in the predawn light.

Gradually other passengers began coming onto the deck. Before long the deck filled with people. Some engaged in one of my favorite past times quietly watching the sea roll past. Others talked with friends and family members. Children played and laughed together. The morning light grew in intensity as did life on the ship; giving truth to the saying that with light there is life. Gradually the sun burned off the haze revealing a beautiful, cloudless day.

At the breakwater

Waiting to enter the port

Dalian

everal hours passed. I suddenly noticed a large ship off to our right. Then I saw another and another and in the distance even more ships of various sizes and realized this is the "parking lot" for ships waiting to go into Dalian's port. I had never seen so many ships in one place. As far as I could see, ships were riding at anchor waiting their turn to enter the port. I wondered how long a ship usually waits to enter.

Off the ship

As we rounded the point of the peninsula earlier, I had noticed the ship turning north. I turned and to my surprise saw land rising steeply from the sea's edge forming small hills on the horizon. "Wow!" I thought, "The land really slipped up on me." The anchored ships had been so interesting that I hadn't turned around for fifteen or twenty minutes. For some reason, perhaps Florida, I had assumed the peninsula would be flat.

I overheard the word, 'Loshun' spoken several times and saw fellow passengers pointing toward the shore. Later I learned that Loshun is the first town or city of any size on the peninsula. Dalian lay approximately two hours away further north.

I stood on the deck looking at the parked ships on one side. Then I turned and watched the shore slide past on the other side. As we approached Dalian, industrial plants became numerous along the shore. Gradually downtown Dalian came into view. A long breakwater extended in a curve outward from the shore. Passing the opening in the breakwater our ship slowly moved into the harbor. Here, as in Hangu, workers scurried around the docks; cranes, in continuous motion, loaded and unloaded ships and trucks moved in and out of the dock areas.

Suddenly I heard a familiar voice behind me. "Hello! I hope you had a good night's sleep!"

I turned and saw it was the man who had helped me the day before board the ship. "Yes," I replied, "I did. I slept much better than I thought I would. The ride was exceptionally smooth."

"Yes," he replied, "we were fortunate. The sea was smooth. It is not always so. Well, I must go. If you need anything, please call me at my university." He gave me his business card.

"I will," I replied. "And thanks again for all your help."

My newfound friend disappeared through the doorway into the ship. I returned my attention to the docking of our ship. I was surprised how quickly the whole operation was carried out. Almost before I realized that we were docked, an announcement came over the shop's intercom. I knew the meaning of the message. Passengers all around me began picking up their suitcases, bags and belongings and started crowding toward the gangplank.

"I see no reason to rush," I told myself. I never desire ending up in the middle of a crowd pushing their way to the gangplank of the ship. After all I thought, "Matt won't leave if I'm not among the first off the ship."

Matt, his wife, Elaine, and their two daughters, Kate and Maggie, lived at the Maritime University where he was studying Chinese. If all went well, he planned to start a business and live in Dalian for years to come.

Within five or ten minutes the ship was quite clear of people, and I made my way to the gangplank. Backpack on my back, I walked down the metal gangplank and followed fellow travelers to waiting buses and a three-minute ride to the terminal. No one entered the terminal. I was surprised no one checked my ticket. Following others, I walked across the dock to a small doorway cut through a corrugated metal wall. "I guess," I thought to myself, "this leads to the terminal. It seems a bit strange, but maybe there is a short walk to the terminal door." I stepped through the doorway and found myself on a sidewalk beside a wide, busy street. Surprised that the exit was not into the terminal, but onto a street I thought, "I guess there is no reason a person must walk through a building to exit. This certainly puts people on the street quickly and cuts down on the congestion inside the terminal. Heaven knows, Chinese terminals and train stations are crowded with people just beginning their travel."

Waiting for Matt

Stepping to one side I looked for my American friend, Matt, who was to meet me. He was nowhere in sight. Looking around I saw seven or eight tall construction cranes. High rise buildings were going up all over the city.[viii] I walked the few steps to the street. Stopping and looking to my right I saw that several streets converged forming a large intersection. To my left the street, heavy with traffic, disappeared into the distance. Trucks, buses, taxi cabs and bicycles passed me. It was early morning, but the city was fully awake. The sidewalk was crowded with travelers from the ship and people going to work.

Where is Matt?

"Hmmm," I thought, "I wonder where Matt is this morning?" I have the perpetual hope that people who are to meet me will be waiting when I arrive. This is doubly true when I'm in a city where I speak the language poorly, do not know where I am and do not know in which direction my destination lies. Often my hope was fulfilled, and people were waiting for me, but not this morning.

"Guess I'll just wait," I said to myself. Looking behind me, I saw a wide granite staircase leading to the terminal. "I'll be pretty conspicuous if I stand halfway up the steps," I thought. "I'll be the only white face standing here. I haven't seen another Westerner today. I climbed halfway up the steps, took my backpack off, set it at my feet and looked out over the crowd and traffic. "How long do I wait before I should begin to worry?" I wondered. "Well, I'll give Matt twenty minutes. Then I'll start to worry."

I did not have a map, and this was before the days of the Internet or GPS. I realized that if the university was miles away and there was a traffic jam it could delay Matt an hour or more. Standing on the 'high ground' of the steps I waited with a tinge of discomfort in the pit of my stomach.

Matt and Friends Arrive

Suddenly, to my relief, I saw a long, lanky American striding toward me, hand waving and wearing a big smile on his face. Two young Chinese men, taking two strides for each of Matt's one, valiantly walked, or was it more like a jog, keeping up with him. Relief swelled into my being as I waved my hand in return.

We met at the bottom of the steps giving each other a hug. "Wow," I exclaimed, "it's good to see you."

"Sorry I am a bit late," Matt laughingly said. "It took longer than I expected.

Matt then introduced me to his two friends, Bob and Mike. They were studying English at the university and had adopted the names of Bob and Mike as their "American names." Shaking hands, we greeted each other. Taking western names seemingly was universal for Chinese speakers of English at that time.

Taxi or Bus

Turning to his two friends Matt asked, "Well, what do you think, should take a taxi or a bus to the university?"

"We can take a taxi," one of them said, "but we'll have to watch to be sure the driver doesn't cheat us."

"How much should it cost?" Matt wanted to know.

"About 25 Kwai," Bob said.

"That's right," Mike broke in, "but drivers won't take us for that amount because you two are foreigners. Foreigners always pay more. You're rich you know."

"OK," said Matt, "let's see what they say."

Bob grabbed my backpack from me. "No, no," I said, "I can carry it."

"No!" Bob replied as he grabbed my backpack, "it is my job today." He took the backpack and put it on. Off we went.

"Matt," I said, "don't taxis have meters for the fare?"

"No," he replied. "Not in Dalian. Here we negotiate the fare. Meters would be good. However, I expect taxi drivers would hate them or try to avoid using them. A meter would not let them charge foreigners more or cheat the unaware rider." Matt started walking and talking as we strode down the sidewalk. "Let's find a taxi and see what we can agree on.

Russian Footprints

Down the street we went making our way along the crowded sidewalk. A Chinese woman, at least six feet tall, passed me. "Wow!" I thought, "it is unusual for a Chinese woman to be so tall." Then I saw another almost six feet. Before we reached the square in front of the railway station, I saw several more women of equal height.

"Matt," I said, "I've heard that the people in Northern China are tall. I always thought that just meant taller than those in Southern China, but not so tall by American standards. People are tall here."

Matt laughed, "That's right, they are tall here. You'll see lots of tall people in Dalian. It is surprising, isn't it?

"It sure is," I replied.

Matt replied, "Russian influence. Dalian was a Russian treaty port back in the days of imperialism.

"No, it is people growing tall to get sunshine," chimed in Bob. "We have short days here in the winter."

Later I was told that the tall connection between Russians and the tall women and men is Dalian is called, 'Russian footprints.

Taxi Driver

By now, we'd reached the square. Traffic buzzed by. A line of taxis sat waiting. Matt approached a taxi, the first in a line. Speaking halting Chinese, he asked the driver, "How much to The Maritime University."

The driver replied in rapid-fire Chinese. "WHAT DID HE SAY!" Matt asked in an incredulous voice.

Mike spoke up, "He said fifty kwai."

"No way," Matt said indignantly, throwing up his hands. "Tell him no more than twenty-five!"

Mike relayed the message. The driver laughed and spoke rapidly again.

"Mike, what did he say?" Matt asked.

Mike waved his hand in disgust, "He said foreigners pay more."

"Forget him!" Matt said. "Let's ask another driver."

I followed along after the trio to another taxi. Different taxi, same story only this driver only wanted forty-five kwai.

"Forget the taxis," Matt said, "let's take a bus. It will cost a lot less with no hassle. I should take the taxi's license tags down and turn them in to the authorities. It's supposed to be against the law to charge foreigners more. Taxi drivers make me so mad." With a final wave of distaste, Matt exclaimed, "Let's go!"

Walking several blocks through the crowds, traffic and rising heat, we made our way to a bus stop. Luck was with us. In less than five minutes, a bus lumbered down the street, blue smoke billowing from its tailpipe.

"That's our bus," Bob shouted.

The Bus

The bus stopped in front of us. The doors opened. A flood of people streamed forth from the back door. Once the river of people slowed to a trickle, We, being good natives by this time, shoved our way onto the bus. No polite standing around waiting our turn for us. To be polite is to be left standing at the curb when the bus pulls away.

Matt called over his shoulder, "Don't worry Bill, I'll take care of the fare."

We pushed our way onto the back of the bus. Giving an extra shove, I made it and my backpack onto the bus. Without the extra shove, my backpack would not have allowed the doors to close. Looking around, I saw there were no seats available There I stood in bodily contact on all sides, a normal situation on a Chinese city bus.

At the next three stops, more people got off the bus than came on board. We were heading away from the city center. There was still no room for us to sit. The tiny ticket agent squirmed her way through the crowd selling bus tickets. It was a marvel as she slipped in, around, and passed people while collecting money and handing out slips of paper. I never understood how ticket sellers on crowded Chinese buses remember who had bought tickets and who had not.

Holding the overhead handrail, we talked as the bus rolled through the streets of Dalian. Bending down, I watched the city as we went past. Dalian, like Tianjin, had been a treaty port and had more of a European look than most Chinese cities.

"Look at the buildings," Matt called to me. "Look at that architecture."

I looked. Indeed, the buildings had a decided Russian appearance. It was not the ugly Russian Communist cement apartment buildings now seen throughout China. Rather these were leftovers from the Czarist days when "The Great Game" of carving up China was in full swing among European nations. Red brick with woven patterns of black brick gave the buildings an interesting, appealing appearance. What hopes and dreams must have taken place in these buildings during that time of colonialism.

The Russians were not the only ones who left images of the West in Dalian. Watching buildings roll past through the bus window, I was surprised and exclaimed, "Those are Tudor style buildings." The white walls with the designs of oak timbers made it easy to make this identification. Perhaps I should not have been surprised after being in Tianjin, but surprised I was to see these European-style buildings.

Gradually, the city gave way to small villages. The bus climbed over small hills that dotted the landscape. Their steep sides and rounded tops reminded me of the small volcanic cone hills that dot the Shenandoah Valley of Virginia. Dropping down the other side of the mountain, Matt looked back calling to me, "We'll get off at the second stop. I need to buy bread at a bakery. Then we will catch a minibus to the university."

"OK" I called back, "I'll follow."

Matt explained about minibuses. "They're privately owned," he said, "and drive the same routes as the city buses."

The piqued my curiosity, "You mean they compete with the city buses?"

"Yes," he replied, "they cost more, but are quicker and you don't have to stand."

Laughing, I said, "That would not be allowed in the States. Gee, China is more Capitalistic than the USA." I was not serious.

The bus pulled to a stop and the four of us got off. Matt approached me. "We will catch the minibus here. We are about ten minutes from the university."

Walking along the street I was surprised when Matt turned and entered a Holiday Inn. "The bakery is here," he said. I think he had noticed the puzzled look on my face.

A Holiday Inn looks like a Holiday Inn all over the world but not all have bakeries. Some smart manager realized that both travelers and expats were potential customers for Western pastries and breads. The pastries were tempting, and there were several kinds of bread to buy. Matt made his purchases. Then we walked outside to wait for a minibus. Climbing aboard the first to come to the stop, we were on the final leg of our trip to the Maritime University. Ten minutes later, we exited the minibus. Looking around I saw we were at a free market. Vegetables and meats sat in the open air. Clothing hung on clotheslines. The smell of cooking street foods and charcoal filled my nose. Cooked meat on skewers lay beside charcoal grills. The meat looked and smelled like a good snack but being cautious I never sampled any such food. A small crowd milled around bargaining and buying goods and snacks.

"Come on," Matt called. "Let's get home in time for lunch."

We walked on the side of the road in the direction the bus had driven, the din of life assaulting our ears. Ahead was a bridge. As we crossed the bridge a foul smell entered our noses and evil looking black water greeted our eyes. Tall marsh grass and cattails grew along the stream's edge. To me this was surprising. The water appeared far too polluted for anything to live. If any fish lived in this water, I surely did not want them for my lunch or supper.

A hundred or so yards beyond the stream we turned right and entered the gates of the Maritime University. Matt and Elaine were busy with classes leaving no time for sightseeing. I babysat their two daughters during the day. They were good kids, so it was no problem. In the evening, we sat and talked. I saw little of Matt and Elaine as there were busy with classes and caring for their two daughters, Kate and Maggie. Several days I was there I took care of the girls.

There was always a cool breeze from the ocean. Opening the front door and windows on the other side created a nice breeze that blew through the apartment.

Seafood Market

One day Matt asked me if I would go to the market with him. I was interested as I have never visited one in China. As I expected an abundance of seafood was on display, crabs, squid, shellfish, and many varieties of fish. Cooked squid on a stick was a new sight for me. Also, there was pork, a variety of fruit and vegetables as well as varieties of tofu. Matt's primary goal was to buy milk and eggs. His Chinese is becoming fluent, and it was interesting watching him bargain with the various vendors.

Kate

Kate, the eldest daughter was five. While I was there, she was in the "I hate everything Chinese" phase. I thought this a normal stage and knew that, in time, she would accommodate herself to China. This process was a big adjustment for a small girl.

Two days a week Kate goes to day-care. At other times during the week a Chinese lady cares for Kate and Maggie while Matt and Elaine are in school and while they study in the afternoon. She also washes their clothes and does other odd jobs. Elaine said the lady does not have to do these jobs but wants to help. Elaise said, "She is a real answer to prayer."

Piles of Dirt

In an open field outside the apartment window there was an open field with evenly spaced piles of dirt. Every day more dirt was brought in and added. Herein lies a mystery. Workers moved dirt from one pile to another and then moved that pile back to its original location. I could not figure out their plan or if there was a plan. I could see no discernable progress. Everything was done by hand requiring many workers.

Impressions

During my days in Dalian, I noticed many of the people were very light skinned, much fairer than in other parts of China I had visited. Also, as I mentioned before, the people were taller than in southern China.

Many of the young women wore very short, tight leatherette skirts. I had not seen women dressed this way in Beijing or Tianjin. Young women who worked in offices wore business suits. Helena told me they were called 'white collar girls.' And that young women who worked in factories were called 'blue collar girls.'

Return to Tianjin

Train Ticket

Several days passed and it was time for me to return to Tianjin. One of Matt's friends told him there was a daily train from Dalian, leaving at 9:00p.m. and arriving in Tianjin at 11:00a.m. the next day.

Matt introduced me to a young friend William who had a cousin who worked at the information booth in the Dalian train station. The train was scheduled to leave Dalian at 9:00 p.m. and arrive in Tianjin in the afternoon the next day.

"My cousin can help you," William said. "I called her about the train and told her about you. We can go to the station and talk with her, find out what we need to do."

She was on duty at an information window when we arrived. William introduced me to her. As we talked, she was interrupted by several telephone calls. Obviously, she was a busy lady. William had quánshì[ix] with his cousin because he was her relative. I was fortunate.

William and his cousin talked for a few minutes. Then William turned to me, she said to give her the money. She would buy the ticket and have it here for us tomorrow.

William turned to me and said, "If there is an additional cost she will cover it and you can pay her when we pick up the ticket." I gave her the money and thanked her. Then William and I left to join Matt and two of his friends.

This was an example of how useful contacts or persons with power and influence (quánshì) are in China. Life is much easier if you have quánshì or know someone who has quánshì.

The next day, a Saturday, was supposed to be a sports day at the university and classes were cancelled. Heavy rain fell during the night. The sports day was cancelled, and classes were to be held. Elaine and Matt were disappointed as they had looked forward to a day off to be with me on my last day.

Soft Sleeper Compartment

To help me Elaine packed some fruit and food for me to eat on the train. She also gave me three packets of instant cereal that contained the cereal, a sweetener, and powdered milk. Hot water in large thermos bottles was always available in a soft-sleeper department. I was ready for the return trip to Tianjin.

Matt and three of his young friends accompanied me to the train station. We arrived about 8:15 p.m. and picked up my ticket. Then we walked to the soft sleeper waiting room and its sofa chairs. Others waited to board the train.

On the Train

At 8:40 the boarding announcement sounded over the loudspeakers. We said goodbye and I followed other travelers and boarded the train. I stowed my backpack and sat down. At 9:00, as scheduled, the train began moving. My next stop was Tianjin.

Soft-sleeper compartments, the Chinese first class service, were compartments with four bunks, two lower and two higher. The lower bunk was high enough off the floor that a suitcase could be slid under it for storage. Above the door was a shelf large enough to hold a suitcase. I had a lower bunk. Between the lower bunks under the window was a small fold-down table. Under the table were two large thermos bottles that were always kept full by the car attendant.

In my compartment were a Korean businessman and a Chinese couple. The Chinese woman spoke no English. Her husband spoke a little English as did the Korean man. I spoke a little Chinese. The businessman spoke no Chinese. This was somewhat surprising as he said he had lived in China for six years. In an hour or so the businessman and couple got off the train and we were joined by a Chinese couple and their daughter who was using crutches. The crutches were a mystery to me. When sitting or lying down she could move her legs with no problem but appeared to have no muscle strength or control when she stood. My guess was she was ten or eleven years old. Most of the time she read magazines. This family of three got off the next morning. A man and his wife entered the compartment and settled down. As soon as the train began moving the man opened a plastic bag, removed food and began eating. I do not remember if his wife ate anything, but he ate continuously until we arrived in Tianjin. This included eating a whole roasted duck. I was disgusted at the gluttony and could not imagine where he put all that food.

Because Dalian is on the Liaotung peninsula, the train traveled north to Shenyang, the capital of Liaoning Provence before turning south toward Tianjin. When I woke up, we were headed south. I could see the green shoots of winter wheat, just a few inches high growing. Further south it was about waist high.

It seemed obvious to me that this area was once under an ocean. When the rail line went through a cut in a hill, I could see shale and granite. Other hills looked like small Teton mountains with small pine trees. Near the rail line Cottonwood trees grew. As the train rolled past villages, I saw onions, cabbages, lettuce, and pole beans growing in gardens. Many trees leaned toward the north showing that strong winds blow here. I know there is logging to the north in Heilongjiang province and in Siberia. There were flat freight cars loaded with logs that were primarily oak and white birch. This was the only time in all my travels in China that I saw freight cars loaded with logs.

Arrival in Tianjin

Bright sunshine greeted us when the train arrived at 4:45 p.m. in Tianjin. I got off and walked into the station and saw no familiar faces. Seeing a shady spot just outside the train station I walked there to wait. In a minute or two I saw Li and her son. They came running up.

"We missed you inside," she said. "We will catch a taxi home."

Walking to a line of yellow breadbox taxis we went in the one that was first in line. In twenty or thirty minutes we were at the Tianjin Normal University where I checked in and was given room no. 223.

"We will come back at six and go to my mother's apartment for supper," she said.

During the evening meal Li said, "I have a friend who is the manager of a four-star hotel. He bought your ticket to Hefei. Without his help it would have been impossible. There is only one train a day. It begins in Beijing and only four tickets are reserved for travelers from Tianjin." Again, it is good to have friends who have quánshì with others who can help.

I was back in my room by 8:00 p.m. and as I was tired went to bed.

Tianjin to Hefei

Train Station

Harvesting wheat

It was time to leave Tianjin and travel to Hefei in Anhui Province to visit the parents of Jing Wang who was living with us in Annapolis while attending St. John's College. Li Zhi called them the day before I was to leave, giving them my travel schedule. They said Jing's father would meet the train.

Li went with me to the station. I believe it was the old Tianjin West Station, architecturally a European looking building. The station was small as was the waiting room. Obviously, it dated -back to the period when Tianjin was a treaty port, 1860-1902. The waiting room was freshly painted, an off-white with green trim. The chairs were comfortable, nothing like the wooden benches in the larger stations. It was the nicest station I saw in China.

The train did not pull in on schedule. Laughing I said, "Well, today we have a ticket but no train."

Li laughed and agreed.

The train pulled into the station ten minutes late. Saying goodbye to Li, I walked to the platform, found the car I needed, climbed aboard and then walked to the compartment and berth assigned and printed on my ticket. As the train pulled out, I saw we were now nine minutes late, a pickup of one minute. Leaving the city, the train rolled directly to the south.

On the train

Soon we were rolling through the countryside. Though it was late May I was surprised to see some wheat showed a golden blush, the promise of a harvest soon to be gathered. When we entered Anhui Province, the fields were a golden yellow, being harvested. I wrongly believed that the fields would all be rice paddies this far south. As the train rolled south, fields of wheat gave way to green paddies of rice that would be harvested later in the summer.

The first hour or so the ride was bumpy. It was obvious that there was a need for track maintenance. Then the rails became smooth. There was no click-clack, all rail noise disappeared, and I realized we were on tracks with welded joints. The train was now smooth and quiet. Sometime during the night, the welded connections ended, and I again heard the click-clack sound. It may have roused me from sleep, but soon put me to sleep again.

Fellow Travelers

Three young men shared the compartment with me. One said he spoke a little English. The other two said they spoke no English. The conversation was, thus, limited. Somewhere during the night, the English speaker got off the train. The two non-English speakers traveled on to Hefei.

Hefei

Arrival

We arrived in Hefei at 7:40 a.m., a bright, sunny morning. Jing's father was on the platform waiting. He had a photo of me that Jing or Nancy had sent. I believe I was the only foreigner on the train. He recognized me as soon as he saw me. We made our way to the terminal, one of the smallest I saw in China. Catching a taxi, we were soon at his apartment where his wife had breakfast waiting for us.

After eating Wang turned and said, "I need your passport. I need to show the police a foreigner is staying with us."

"Do I need to go with you?" I asked.

"No, you stay here and rest," he said.

I gave him my passport and he left to do his duty. Soon he returned. Smiling he returned my passport. "OK," he said. Let's take a walk. We left the apartment and had walked only a few steps when rain began to fall.

"Let's go back," he said.

Just as we entered the apartment the rain turned into a deluge that lasted fifteen or twenty minutes. Wang shook his head, "I was hoping I could take you to Huang Shan, the Yellow Mountain. That is a bad idea now. This is the beginning of the wet season. Sometimes they come earlier than now and sometimes later. If we went, we would not see anything. With the rain it becomes foggy. It would not be a good trip."

Morning

Across the street from the apartment was the end of a lake surrounded by a park with walking trails, trees, flowers, and plants. Jing's mom took me to the park on my first day with them. While there she introduced me to some of her friends and coworkers. People had gathered in groups, some to dance with fans, do aerobic dancing, qi gong, or tai chi. Old men brought their caged birds which they hung in trees and then sat listening to their birds sing. Students sat studying. Others were taking their morning walk around the park. I cannot remember all the activities. This type of activity can be seen all over China in the early morning. Parks and empty places are filled with people taking part in activities. Flowers were blooming, spaced along the walkways and in gardens. Tall trees created a forest atmosphere. There were trees from Australia, as well as a type of cypress without knees. Many Black Locust were in bloom. It was a pleasant morning. Finally, we returned to the apartment.

Bao Zheng Memorial

Later in the day Jing's father and one of Jing's friends, Wang Yang and I took a long walk through the park. Toward the far end of the park, we visited a temple dedicated to a famous Chinese mandarin, Bao Zheng. Bao Zheng is remembered, respected, and honored as an example of an honest government official. He hated corruption, and fearlessly punished high officials as well as others. As he had grown up in a poor family, he understood hardships

and was sympathetic to

ward those facing such problems.

Funeral

We walked to a nearby Buddhist temple. Drawing close we saw there was a service in progress. Wang inquired about the service. Turning to me he said, "It is a funeral for an American Chinese man.". His family had returned to Hefei for the ceremony here in the man's ancestral city. We watched for about thirty minutes. "I can't understand anything the monks chant," Wang said. The ceremony was still going when we left to return to the apartment.

Funeral procession

Mingjiao Temple First Beggars

The first beggars I saw were in Hefei. I had seen no beggars when I was in Beijing, Tianjin, or Dalian. I did not take this to mean there were no beggars in those cities. I was sure there were but not where I happened to visit. Later I saw beggars in Xi'an, Nanjing and Guiyang.

My friend, Wang took me to the famous Mingjiao Temple that was built in the sixth century. Outside the entrance to the Four Heavenly Kings Hall several beggars with badly deformed bodies were on their knees, their heads touching the ground with their hands stretched out, palms upward. I noticed as we walked past, Wang dropped a coin into each hand.

The next day a man with hands out begging approached Wang and me. Wang yelled at him, waving him off with both hands. Turning to me Wang said, "He is not a beggar. Did you see his clothes, a new Mao suit? He is a peasant who came to town today, hoping to get some money. I will give money to people who need it, but not to people like him." Wang was a friendly, generous man but he had standards by which he lived his life. I filed this information away in my mind and remembered it later in the summer.

Hefei to Suzhou

Peasant village from the train

Train to Suzhou

Lao Wang sat beside me in the soft seat section of the day train from Hefei to Suzhou. He pointed to the window seat. "Sit here, you will enjoy the countryside," You have not traveled here before. I have many times. You will find it very interesting."

Near us a family carried onboard a metal dishpan filled with eels that they placed on the platform between two cars, near a lavatory. Suddenly there was a commotion. One of the eels had escaped and was squirming rapidly down the aisle. The father jumped up scurrying here and there until he finally caught the eel and returned it to the pan. This incident brought chuckles from other passengers.

With a gentle bump, the train was set in motion. I sat watching the city of Hefei roll past. Soon we were in the Anhui countryside passing peasant villages.

Houses in the peasant villages in this province were formed of sun-dried bricks with a facing of mud mixed with straw. Except for trees, everything in these villages was muddy. Muddy streets ran through the villages. Hard-surfaced streets did not exist. The walls surrounding the villages were the same as the homes.

Later, in Jiangsu, many houses in peasant villages were new government-built or subsidized brick homes.

I mentioned this to Wang. With an expression of sadness, he said, "Anhui is the third world of the third world. So many are poor, and there is little or no hope of improvement. Others are gaining wealth, but not the peasants."

I knew the province of Gansu is called the third world of the third world, but I did not know the same was said of Anhui. "I don't understand," I replied, "the land looks fertile and productive. Why is Anhui so poor?"

Lao Wang thought a moment before answering. "We have no industry in Anhui. We need industry to help the economy."

By mid-morning the sun was high, and the temperature was creeping upward. We opened our window to allow the cool breeze to blow past us. I looked out the window to the rice paddies. Though it was May, the first rice planting was being harvested. Paddies already harvested were being plowed for the second planting. Water buffalo pulled long toothed harrows through the mud. Peasants worked knee deep working the soil. Surely it is hard, unpleasant work.

Rice and a Chinese Problem

Leaning toward me, Lao Wang pointed out the window. "What do you see?" he asked.

"I see old men and women, and a few young women working," I replied.

"That's right!" he exclaimed. "All you see are old men, old women, and just a few others."

"Where are the young men?" I asked though I knew the answer but wanted to continue the discussion.

"They leave to go to the cities," he replied. "No one wants to stay in the countryside."

"Isn't this going to cause a big problem for China?" I asked.

"Yes. I'm very worried about this. In ten or fifteen years, when these people are too old to work—who is going to plant and harvest the rice?" His face was creased with concern. Sighing deeply, he continued, "This is a big problem for China. Life is too hard in the countryside. All the young people want to go to the cities to make money, to live easy." His voice trailed off into silence as we watched the paddies roll past our train. "We have many problems in China," he said breaking the silence, "many problems."

What Would Life Be

I watched in silence. It was very easy for me to see that life was very hard in the countryside of Anhui province. Village after village rolled past as the train slowly made its way. Mentally I asked myself, "What would my life have been like if I had been born in a peasant village in Anhui? My house would be constructed of mud bricks. The earthen floor, mashed flat by the feet of my family, would be all I had ever known. Working the rice paddies every day with no power tools and no tractors would have toughened my muscles. My back, neck, face, and arms all would have burned black in the hot South China sun. My education would have been limited, assuming I was fortunate enough to have received any schooling. I would know and be known well by my fellow villagers. There are no secrets in a peasant village. I would have known each person in the village since birth and would know of their successes, failures, indiscretions, sicknesses, and health. I would distrust others, guarding, if not my thoughts, what I said publicly and to my family. As a witness to so many political movements that turned neighbor against neighbor, son against father, mother against daughter, and sibling against sibling, I would be careful, a movement might begin anytime.

As the train rumbled past village after village, I would gaze intently, trying to catch a glimpse of the interior of a home. Occasionally, a door had been left open and, indeed, I did catch a glimpse. However, the glimpse only whetted my desire to see more. Watching the men and women working in the rice paddies, I slowly realized that I had no background to understand what their life was really like. Thus, I could not truthfully imagine what my life would have been like if I had been born here. I could only speculate, only guess—indeed, this is all even most urban Chinese dwellers could do. My impression is the Chinese urban dweller has no real concept of what it is to be a peasant. It is almost as if there are two races living in the same country, and though they interact in the markets, neither has much understanding of the other. I find it is the same in the United States. City dwellers have no idea of life in the country, and country people have no idea of what life is like in the city. Why would I expect it to be different in China?

"Harvesting the rice looks like such hard work," I said. Men and women were bending, holding short-handled sickles in one hand they grabbed a handful of rice stalks in the other. With a quick motion of the sickle, they cut through the rice. Skillfully, still holding the cut rice, the process was repeated until a bundle of harvested rice filled their left arm. The bundle was then laid on the ground and the process continued.

"It is very hard work," replied Lao Wang shaking his head. "The women are better workers than the men."

I looked at the paddies closely and saw that most of the workers were women. "Why is that?" I wanted to know.

With a shrug, he replied, "The men are lazy."

Nanjing Bridge

The train traveled eastward crossing the famous four-mile-long Nanjing Bridge over the Yangtze River. In the past engineers believed such a bridge was impossible to build. Perhaps they were correct considering the technology of their era. The building of the bridge began in the 1960's and it opened for traffic in 1968. It quickly became the most frequent suicide site in the world averaging one suicide a day. Double-decked, the upper deck carries automobiles while trains cross on the lower level. Young soldiers with automatic weapons guarded both ends. My thought was, "What a boring job."

Suzhou the Venice of China

Suzhou canal

City of Canals

Water Garden

Suzhou is called the Venice of China. Canals run through the city as does the thousand mile long Grand Canal. Boats are still poled from place to place carrying products throughout the city.

In ancient times high government officials retired to Suzhou where they created many 'water gardens.' The houses and water gardens were surrounded by high walls affording privacy and protection.

We got off the train in Suzhou in early evening. I was surprised when Wang led me to a pedicab instead of a taxi. We climbed into the pedicab and off we went. As the man peddled us through the city, he and Wang chatted. Wang was one of those people who are friendly and before long you would have thought the two men had been friends since high school. At that time my Chinese was as good as it every would be. I listened carefully and did not hear a word I recognized. It dawned on me they were speaking the Suzhou dialect, not Mandarin.

The Apartment

Wang knocked on the door. His eldest sister and her husband, Xu, answered the door. Wang introduced me. They were surprised to see us. Wang did not have her new telephone number and had not given her advanced notice of our visit. Warmly greeting us, they invited us in, welcoming us for our three-day stay.

Their just-remodeled apartment was sparkling with new paint and furniture. Spotless newly installed wooden floors, and tile shone. The recessed ceiling with recessed lighting gave a warm glow. The walls were paneled with a color complimenting the floor and ceiling. Had we arrived last week, we could not have stayed with them.

Immediately they invited us to sit in the living room. As we sat around a circular coffee table, Wang's sister set a dish of peanuts in front of us and then went to the kitchen to prepare our evening meal. Eating the peanuts, we had a contest to see who could pick up the most peanuts at one time with chopsticks. There was no clear winner. Picking up two was easy. Picking up three was hard.

Two-Dollar Bill

As we talked Mr. Xu, Wang's brother-in-law, said to me that he had several US bills. He brought them out. I remember he had several one-dollar bills, one or more five-dollar bills and a twenty. I do not remember if he had a fifty or a hundred-dollar bill.

"I have a bill that I will give you," I said. "It is a bill I bet you did not know exists."

"You have me curious," Xu said smiling.

I opened my backpack and took out the bill. "Here, this is for you. It is a two-dollar bill."

"I've never heard of such a bill," he said in a surprised voice.

I handed him the bill, "Not all Americans know about the two-dollar bill. Racetracks use them. I believe that two-dollar bets are the smallest bet a person can make; also, banks use them in transfers between banks. They are seldom used by anyone else."

Slowly Xu looked at both sides of the bill, examining them carefully. Looking up, he smiled, "Thank you, I will keep it in my collection.

We talked, ate our evening meal, and talked until we all headed to bed.

Wailing

I awoke early the next morning and wrote a letter to Nancy. When I heard others moving around, I left my room to join them. During breakfast, Wang told me that today we would visit various places in Suzhou, starting with Tiger Hill.

Leaving the apartment, we made our way along a narrow street and across one of the humpbacked bridges over a canal. As we passed an ancient traditionally built Chinese house, I heard wailing.

"What is that?" I wanted to know.

Pointing his finger Wang said, "Someone has died. It would be a male family member. The wailing is for him."

Walking along I mused out loud, "I have read and heard about professional wailers, but this is the first time I have heard them."

"They are not professional wailers," said Mr. Xu shaking his head. "They are family members."

The wailing had a melodious sound. When I first heard it from a distance, I thought it sounded like some type of choir practice. There seemed to be a lead wailer. This wailer would chant or wail a line or a sentence. Then the other wailers would respond with the same wail.

Xu continued, "These days this is usually only people in the countryside who wail like this. Only women wail. It is seldom we hear traditional wailing in the city."

Considering that this family must be very traditional, I knew they would have a procession with the wailing and all the traditional trappings. Someone carrying a long burning joss stick standing for the soul of the deceased leads the procession. People carry paper cars, airplanes and money signifying the wealth of the family as well as helping the deceased. Food for the dead is included, as they will need nourishment in the afterlife.

We passed on through the city. Our destination was Tiger Hill. First however we made a visit to one of Wang's relatives who managed a five-star hotel. It was located just outside the Tiger Hill entrance.

Black Tea

We entered the hotel's richly decorated lobby. The marble floor was shiny. Large mirrors covered the walls. Strategically overstuffed chairs and sofas created a welcoming atmosphere. Expensive area carpets added to the décor.

Wang's relative met us. After Wang introduced me the two men chatted for a few moments. "Come with me," the manager said. He led us to a small room with plush soft carpet and expensive looking furniture. We sat at a table with four chairs.

Then the hotel manager turned and asked, "Would you like a cup of tea?"

"Yes, that would be nice," I said. I was thirsty.

"Good," he replied, "I will get a cup of tea for each of us."

Soon a server placed three cups and a container of hot water on the table. I was surprised. The tea bag was Lipton Tea. This was the first black tea I had seen in China. I had always been served either green tea or Jasmine tea, never black tea.

Wang picked up the tea bag, looking at it with curiosity. "What tea is this?

"It is black tea," I replied. "This is the type of tea Americans almost always drink. Have you tasted it before?"

"No, never saw it before." He continued inspecting the tea.

We opened the tea bags and placed them in the hot water we'd just poured into our cups. Once waiting a minute or so Wang raised the cup and took a drink.

I wondered what he would think, what his reaction might be. It was not long in coming.

With a quick turn he leaned forward and caught himself just before spitting it onto the hotel carpet. "I no like!" he exclaimed. He swallowed the tea. That was his first and last mouthful of black tea.

Tiger Hill

Pizza has its leaning tower. Suzhou has its leaning pagoda, Yunnan Pagoda. Constructed in the tenth century the lower levels served for seven hundred years. Later, in the seventeenth century the construction of the uppermost levels made a total of seven stories. Over the centuries the pagoda began to lean. Presently the difference between the base and the top is just over six and a half feet. The problem arose because the construction of the base is half on rock and half on dirt.

Lake Tai

We caught a bus to ride to the beautiful lake, Lake Tai, and got off on one of the islands. Sadly, fog obscured our view, and we could see little. On the island we toured a cave, wet with dripping water forming stalactites and stalagmites. Unfortunately, the lights were on continuously. The heat from the lights allowed moss and small plants to grow on some of the stone formations. We spent about an hour touring the cave before leaving and catching a bus.

The fog had burned off and we now had good views of the lake. There were boats on the lake, but none with sails and no traditional Chinese junks. I had hoped to see a junk, but it was not to be. The boats I saw looked to be about thirty feet long and eight feet wide. On the aft end is a cabin where the family lives and occasionally I saw a woman and a child on the deck. Drying clothes hung on lines at the living cabin end of the boat. Their livelihood is made by transporting merchandise from place to place.

The Story of Ping, the white duck came to my mind when I realized I had not seen any ducks on the lake. Did that mean that Ping had been caught and became someone's lunch? I think not.

Buddhist Monastery

I watched the countryside roll past the bus with peasants working in the rice paddies near their homes in the villages. Here the season was ahead of that in Anhui. The workers were bending over weeding the paddies. The sunburned skin and worn, frayed clothing of the people spoke of poverty. I tried to imagine what it would be like to grow up and live in such a village. But I had no background to picture such a life.

Suddenly the bus began slowing and to my surprise Wang got up and motioning with his hand said, "We will get off here."

I was surprised. I thought our next stop would be in Suzhou. Instead, we were getting off in the country, not even in a village. My though was, "Who am I to argue. He knows where we are going. "This is not to say that I was not curious why we got off in the country. I was, but this was an adventure. Right?

Once the bus had pulled off we walked across the road, and I saw a wide, well-maintained path leading toward a small mountain.

I walked with Wang as he led me across the road to a path that disappeared

into a bamboo fores t. Bamboo is one of my favorite plants. Small bamboo that grows only a few inches high or large bamboo that grows up to forty or fifty feet tall, I like them all. The path wound its way up the mountain, and I enjoyed hearing the Bamboo leaves rustle and the stalks click and groan in the breeze. Occasionally a bird fluttered from stalk to stalk going about the daily tasks, picking bugs off the bamboo, living and dying in this beautiful place.

In thirty or forty minutes we arrived at the Wuzhong In thirty or forty minutes we arrived at the Wuzhong Shenjing monastery and temple complex where, to my surprise, we ate lunch. Buddhists are vegetarians so there was no meat.

There also was no menu. Visitors ate the 'food of the day'. This day it was crunchy lotus root with soft soy flavored dofu,[x] three kinds of mushrooms in a mildly spiced butter colored sauce and boiled noodles. Was it good? Well, we had two servings of each.

It seemed strange at the time and still does that I didn't see one Buddhist monk. In fact, I don't remember seeing any other person, not even the person who filled our small plates with food since Wang brought the food to our table from behind frosted glass windows.

After eating we walked through the monastery grounds; a sunken garden with a water lily pond was a delight to my eyes. The lilies were in bloom. Looking closely suddenly I noticed a large green frog and then looking carefully I saw the pond was full of large green frogs and realized they were difficult to see as their green was almost exactly the same green as the leaves of the water lilies.

By now the fog had burned off. Now we could clearly see as we made our way down the mountain, down through the beautiful bamboo forest. Finally, we arrived at the road, the bus stop where we waited, climbed on the next bus and

Rats

It was our last night in Suzhou, and we went by taxi to Wang's oldest sisters' apartment for the night. I was surprised. As we walked to catch a taxi, it seemed that with each step I saw one or more rats scurry out of our path. I had seen rats in Baltimore and Washington, but never had I seen as many rats as in Suzhou. Fortunately, none of them paid any attention to us other than scurrying out of our way. Thank goodness none was aggressive. I wondered what would happen if rabies broke out in the vast population of rats. I also noticed garbage, a rat's favorite food, lying by buildings. It seemed as if Suzhou were a large garbage landfill with buildings.

Scene from the train

Suzhou Back to Hefei

Train from Suzhou Back to Hefei

The train returning to Hefei left Suzhou early in the morning and arrived in Hefei in the afternoon. We all got up at 5:00 a.m., quickly ate a jiaozi breakfast and by 5:30 walked to a nearby street and caught a taxi to the train station. Cleaning ladies were sweeping the large area in front of the station. Others were sweeping the lobby and ticketing area in the station. Outside the station several food stands were open. We bought several packages of food and several bottles of soft drink. We were not going to go hungry this day. The wheels of the train began to turn at 6:20. This train, like the one we had traveled on to Suzhou, was a day train. There were no sleeper cars.

Air Conditioning

Across the aisle was a young couple from Taiwan. By 8:00 heat began to build, making the car uncomfortable. Wang motioned to the car attendant. "Turn on the air conditioning," he said. "There are foreigners riding and they paid a lot of money for their tickets. That includes air conditioning, and it should be turned on. Do you want them to think we are so backward that we do not have air conditioning?" Soon cool air began blowing through the car. Smiling, Wang said, "If there were only Chinese on the car, they would not turn it on."

Listening In

The couple talked with a retired mainland China couple. The husband now retired, had been the warden of a prison. He and his wife were traveling to visit a son. A lively conversation, covering many subjects, continuing between the couples lasted throughout the trip. Wang translated the conversation as best he could.

One discussion centered on the young couple's unfortunate experience with a dishonest taxi driver. This was not an uncommon event in China at that time. Yes, there are regulations governing taxi drivers and fares, but they are ignored all too often. Their conversation went something like this:

The young man, "Taxi drivers are terrible in China, always trying to cheat people."

The older man lifted his hands, "Are they really so bad?"

"Oh, yes. Yesterday we arrived. We got a taxi. I told him the hotel where we had a room reserved. I had no idea how far we were from the hotel. Well, the driver drove and drove and drove and drove, around and around and around.

Half an hour later, he pulled up to the hotel. After paying him, I looked around and realized the train station was only two or three blocks away. I was truly angry, but what could I do?"

"The driver should not have done that," the older man admitted. "We have regulations on this."

The young man laughed, "But not enforced." The discussion continued until the older man and his wife got off the train.

In late afternoon the train arrived in Hefei. We exited the train and took a taxi to Wang's apartment and called it a day.

Rolling across Shaanxi Provence

Hefei to Xi'an

Rush to the Train

Wang rushed into the apartment. "We have to get your ticket to Xi'an," he said. "There is a train this evening, but not tomorrow. The train to Xi'an is every other day."

I cannot remember if I went with Wang to the train station or if he took care of it himself. Regardless, the ticket was bought, I packed, and we were at the station in time for me to be on the train as it left Hefei at 5:30 p.m. that evening. As usual, I was in a soft-sleeper compartment with three Chinese men. Often there is a mix of women and men in a compartment. Whether or not they know each other is not a consideration. The three men were dressed in work clothing. They were workers, not businessmen. None spoke any English. I stowed my backpack under one of the lower bunks that had been assigned to me.

The men talked and laughed incessantly. One, a tall, lean man, dominated the conversation and must have been somewhat of a comedian as he drew much

Watching the countryside roll past the train

laughter. I was totally ignored and that was fine with me. We were together until I arrived in Xi'an the next day at 1:35 p.m. some twenty hours after leaving Hefei.

Friendly man

I slept well during the night. The sun shone brightly as the train traveled.

When travelling by train I liked to stand in the aisle outside the compartment and watch the landscape roll past. Spaced between each window has a pull-down seat. Occasionally, I used the seat, but most of the time, I stood. Regardless of whether it was landscape, village, or city passing, it was fascinating to me. As I stood in the aisle watching the countryside roll past, a man walked down the aisle and stopped beside me.

"May I practice my English?"

I turned and saw a middle-aged man in a business suit. "Oh, yes," I replied. I was not surprised as this had happened before.

"Where are you from?"

"America," I replied.

"Are you traveling alone?"

"Yes, I am."

"Oh," he exclaimed, "You Americas are so bold. But here in China, I believe you are safe."

Smiling I replied, "Yes, I think you are right."

We talked for several minutes before he excused himself and returned to his compartment.

Hua Shan

Mid-morning the train stopped. I decided to get off and stretch my legs by walking on the platform. As I stepped onto the platform, I looked up. Towering over the town was a huge mountain, almost bare of trees. It looked like a huge granite rock, and I realized it was the mountain named Hua Shan. People like to travel to this town and climb the mountain at night so they can watch the sunrise in the morning. Looking at it, I realized the climb must be exhausting and dangerous. I read that at least one hundred people plunge to their deaths each year climbing this mountain. Several times friends have told Nancy and me, "You should climb Hua Shan, people die there every year." I was never sure how I should take this advice.

Northwestern Polytechnical University

NPU Guesthouse Entrance

Arrival at NPU

The train arrived at the Xi'an train station at 1:35 p.m. Gathering my backpack I exited the train. Waiting for me on the platform was Qian Fupei, the man I was to work with, his wife, Yi Ying and two friends, Liu Shengwu and Liu Songling. A young man I did not know was with them.

Qian Fupei introduced the young man, "This is Xiao Ou. He is in my department at NPU, (Northwestern Polytech University).

"Did my suitcase arrive?" I hoped it had.

"Yes," Fupei said, "it is at my apartment."

"That is good," I replied. "I will get it and take it to my room."

Together, we walked out of the station. A university van and driver waited for us. Off we went through the city. The driver drove along the northern part of the city wall. The oldest part of Xi'an is surrounded by a city wall built during

95

the Ming dynasty, 1368 to 1644. Xi'an is the only city left in China with a complete wall around the oldest part of the city.

The van entered the South Gate of the university and let us out beside the building where Fupei and Yi Ying live. After a quick lunch Fupei showed me my suitcase. I was surprised as it was wrapped in plastic. It was as heavy as I remembered. How thankful I was that Dang He's assistants had shipped it by train to Xi'an. We walked to the university guest house where I checked in and was given room 204.

My room

My Room

My room, 204, was on the second floor of the university guesthouse. From the lobby, I had to climb two flights of stairs and turn left down a hallway. A young woman sat at a small desk just to the right of the head of the stairway. Her job was to keep all the thermos bottles in the room supplied with hot water and watch the going and coming of guests. She also took care of any laundry I gave her. To me, it seemed a terribly boring job. She spoke no English and ignored me whenever I walked past. I spoke just enough Chinese to ask for water. That was our only real interaction during the months I was there.

Guestrooms at the university were luxurious compared to the housing for faculty and students. I had a small table with two drawers between two twin beds, two sofa chairs, an air-conditioner, a small refrigerator, and a television set. To my relief, I also had a private toilet and tub. There was a long counter. Below were drawers for clothing. A small TV sat on the counter. The counter also served as my desk. There was no office where I could work. A desktop computer and a dot matrix printer were brought to my room and placed on the counter at the foot of one bed. I edited the papers which were on floppy disks. I quickly learned to check each disk for virus infections before opening the files. Every disk I checked was virus infected. In addition to the viruses, I never saw a legal piece of software. The Microsoft Word program on the computer was registered to a man in Nanjing. I wondered how many computers this program had been installed on before reaching Xi'an.

Three large windows, facing South of East on the outside wall gave me a view of a new building under construction and brought light in over my left shoulder. The blackout curtains I pulled over the windows at night blocked outside light.

Monday to Friday my work schedule was mine to set as I wished. After showering and eating breakfast, I would turn on the computer, sit on the end of the bed, and set to work. On the bed? Yes, there was no room for a chair between the bed and counter, so my knees were smashed into the drawers. This was not exactly a luxurious 'office'. On Saturdays I often went to the city inside the Ming wall and wandered around with no set destination.

Occasionally, I would walk around the campus at mid-morning to shake the cobwebs out of my brain. At noon I would take a lunch break. I ate at the university restaurant for free the first week or two. However, I grew tired of the lack of variety. Within two weeks I had met two or three expats and had made friends with several young Chinese professors. I will write more about the most frequented restaurants later. Afternoons were a repeat of the mornings. In the evenings, I met my friends again and we ate supper off campus. Once back in my room, I stayed up until 9:00 to watch the news in English and then would head to bed.

My Work

My primary job was to take conference papers from Chinese scholars and engineers and edit the English translations. A sample of titles:

1. A Model for Project Selection with Interactions of Multiple Objectives.

2. Project and Practice for Proprietor Management on the Second Phase Construction of Pan Zhi Hua Iron and Steel Company.
3. Preliminary Research for Government Functions and Fundamental Laws Applying to State Large-Scale Project Management.
4. Program Management Decision Making Support Software. (PMDSS).

The translations ran from very good to very poor. At times I needed help with the difficult papers. Qian Fupei and a young professor, Zhou Li Ping, would sit beside me, with the original paper in Chinese, and help me understand what was being said.

Occasionally I was asked to edit an announcement or other small document. This request was made several times by the Waiban (Foreign Affairs Office). Three or four times during the summer, meetings were held in my room reviewing where we were and what still needed to be done.

Once the papers were all edited, I had nothing I needed to do. This gave me time to read and to explore Xi'an.

NPU Library

Shaanxi Opera

Three Drops of Blood

Professor Dong was a friend Nancy and I made in 1987 when he was a visiting scholar at the University of Maryland. Departments in Chinese universities had two deans, an academic and a political dean. Professor Dong was the political dean in the English Department. He was the one who passed information from the Communist Party on to others and had the power to reward or punish department members. I never pressed him on how punishment or reward were decided.

Several times during my six months at Northwestern Polytech University, he invited me to eat lunch in his apartment with him and his wife. She never had a chance to go to school and was unable to read or write. In my opinion she was a Ph.D. in cooking. She always prepared a traditional Shaanxi meal of noodles or a pasta-like food with sauce and vegetables on the side.

One day, after eating, Dong and I sat talking. He said, "Would you like to go to the Shaanxi Opera with me? The opera "Three Drops of Blood" will be performed next week.

"Yes," I replied, "I would like that." Professor Dong loved Shaanxi Opera. He told Nancy and me about this while in the States visiting us. One of us had asked, "What is the difference between Beijing Opera and Shaanxi Opera?"

Laughing, he said, "Shaanxi Opera is noisier."

"I will get tickets," he said. "We will go next Tuesday."

Tuesday arrived. Professor Dong came to my room, and we walked to the South gate of the university and caught a taxi. The theater was in the oldest section of Xi'an, inside the Ming Wall. It was a modern building with a large auditorium full of opera goers.

The story is more or less this: To settle a family quarrel three drops of blood were squeezed from the finger of two men into a glass of water. If the blood merged, it would prove they were relatives. If the blood did not merge, they were not relatives. On the third try, the blood merged, and the opera ended. I am not sure if everyone in the family was happy or not.

I enjoyed the opera, the music, and the costumes, even though I had no idea of what was going on at any given time. Occasionally, Dong would whisper to me what was happening. After the opera was over, we slowly made our way out of the theater. The theater had been filled and it was a slow process leaving the building. This was not a problem as we were in no hurry. Buses ran late and even if there were no buses, there were always taxis.

Golden Lilies or Bound Feet

As we neared the door, I noticed two young women supporting an elderly woman as they approached the exit. Then I saw the elderly women's feet were bound. I knew this meant that before she was nine years old, her toes had been forced under the arch of her feet and bound, creating what are called Lotus Feet. Very possibly bones were broken to do this. Thus, she had lived her life in pain, with small. bound feet. Now, she could not walk without help. Never had she been able to walk normally.

She was the only person I saw with 'golden lilies' in 1995 and I saw none in 2000 when Nancy and I worked at NPU. In 1992 Nancy and I had seen the bound feet of the grandmother of one of our friends. She was elderly and could not walk without help.

Xi'an

Every time I visited the Terra Cotta Warriors
I looked for this thin chariot driver

The Drum Tower

The Drum Tower from the Bell Tower

The tunnel through the tower leads to the Muslim quarter in the old city of Xi'an. One block off West Street all traffic, both vehicular and pedestrian must pass through this tunnel when using this street. The sound of a horn, an all-too-common occurrence, is deafening when walking through the tunnel. I have yet to find a spot from which a good picture of the complete building can be taken. Finally, while visiting the Bell Tower I saw the Drum Tower and snapped a photo. Between these two ancient buildings is an underground upscale shopping mall. Once through the tunnel a world built to remove money from the tourist is encountered. Rather aggressive "art students" approach "inviting" the "foreign friend" into their school's store. The pictures are not original in the sense that each is of a different scene. Rather hundreds of copies of old master's works, or near master's works, or "cute pictures" are for sale.

Drums in the Drum Tower

Tunnel through the Drum Tower

The roof line of the Drum Tower clearly shows the traditional architecture of ancient China. The upturned corners and the figurines discouraged devils from sitting on the roof and watching for victims. I must say they would be quite uncomfortable to use as a seat. The tiles and gray bricks are also common on the older buildings all over China. I had no idea bricks had been in use for such a long period of time in China. My impression was that wood was more commonly used. However, if wood had been used more widely, many of the old structures still to be seen would have long since fallen to fire or lack of maintenance. Brick is much more durable in this regard.

The Drum in the tower was used to announce that evening had arrived, or to announce that an enemy was approaching the city, a call to arms for the defense of the city.

Great Mosque

Street on the way to the Great Mosque.

Great Mosque Prayer Hall

Xi'an is home to a large number of Muslims who have been living there since the time of the Silk Road trade route. Half a block beyond the tunnel was a small, narrow, awning covered street going to the Great Mosque. There was room only for walkers here. Small shops were filled with "stuff" spilling out over the sidewalk. To me there was nothing to buy.

Antique-looking merchandise was not antique but rather mass-produced items that appeared old. I saw a knife in a fancy curved scabbard that looked ancient. At first look I thought this was true. Then I noticed that this knife was on sale by many of the street vendors. There was nothing old about it.

Occasionally I would go to the Great Mosque. It was a place in Xi'an I knew would be quiet. Stepping through the entrance gate quiet greeted me,

no vendor

Modern mosque

pleas, no street noise, just welcome quiet. The grounds were neat and clean with grass growing in the yard. No food wrappers lying on the ground.

The architecture is Chinese, not middle eastern. The only sign that this was not a Confucian temple were the Arabic characters on various walls.

Dry and Hot Summer

The summer of 1995 was a hot and dry summer in Xi'an and Shaanxi Provence. In late October the weather turned cold and wet. The day I left, beginning my trip home, rain threatened and began falling after I was on the train heading to Tianjin. Night after night all summer the English weather on TV reported Xi'an as the hottest city in China. Day after day the high was reported at thirty-nine or forty degrees centigrade. Forty is equivalent to 104 degrees Fahrenheit. One of my friends said the law was that if the temperature rose above 40C all workers were to be sent home. There were days when forty did not feel too hot. There were others where the same temperature felt beastly.

My suspicion was that the government did not want workers to be sent home and, thus, the official temperature never went above the magic number in weather reports on TV.

With the sun beating down constantly and with few clouds in the sky the humidity was low. When I walked in the shade, the heat was not troublesome. That was not true when I was in the sunshine. When walking in the sunshine, I felt as if I were melting like butter and would end up being just a grease spot.

Water became scarce in many areas. Several villages ran completely out of water, and it was not long before tempers began flaring between the villages without water and nearby villages that had water but did not want to share. I was told that fights between peasants broke out. We humans cannot go long without water.

The university depended on two deep wells and to conserve what they had it was available to the campus only at certain hours of the day. There was fear that this would not be sufficient in the future and two new wells were being dug. I never saw or heard the drilling rigs. Water was hit. However, it was hot water not cold. Though totally unexpected this hot water proved to be a blessing. When Nancy and I lived at NPU in 2000, hot water radiators were being installed in the university staff apartments. There had never been central heating of any kind prior to this. The only heat in living quarters had been with charcoal briquettes which were the source of fire for cooking. The briquettes had been strictly rationed meaning most apartments stayed the same temperature inside as the air outside except those with south-facing windows which briefly warmed up a bit during cold weather.

Guangren Temple - Interesting Discovery

Buddha

One Saturday, I decided to explore the Muslim Quarter of Xi'an. I rode the bus to the Bell Tower and then walked to the Drum Tower. Once I had walked through the Drum Tower tunnel, I was in the Muslim Quarter. Street vendors, restaurants, and shops lined the street. The Muslims, a recognized minority group, were always friendly. Though I was the only Westerner there; I did not worry. I arrived at about nine o'clock. There was little activity. Except for the way the people were dressed, there was nothing to show that this was not a normal Chinese street. I had no fear of being lost. I was inside the Ming wall and knew that I could always strike out in any direction and in time I would come to the wall. During my wandering, I saw a modern looking mosque with a dome. I do not know why, but it surprised me. Assuming is usually not smart. It was then that I realized that not all the Muslims in Xi'an would go to one mosque.

I came to the northwest corner of the Ming wall and was surprised to see the entrance to a Buddhist temple. I had passed a domed mosque and would not have been surprised if I had found another. But a Buddhist temple? That was a surprise.

The gate was open, and I entered. The temple complex was surrounded by a wall with one entrance facing South. Immediately, I realized this was a working temple, not one that tried to attract tourists. During my visit, I saw no other Westerners. Indeed, the only people I saw were a few monks. There may be differences between Tibetan temples and Chinese temples but, if so, I could not see them. To me the construction and statues were the same as in other temples I visited. It was years later that I discovered the Guangren temple was a Tibian temple.

The next week I was talking with a friend, Liu Shengwu, and I told him about the temple. "I've never heard of it," he said. Shengwu was a retired professor and had lived in Xi'an for decades.

"Would you like to visit it?" I asked.

"Yes," he replied.

"OK," I said. "We can go on Saturday morning. Meet me in my room at 9:00 and I can take you."

Saturday Morning Visit

Liu Shengwu came to my room just as planned that Saturday. We walked out of the South Gate of the university and caught a city bus to the Bell Tower. From there, we walked to the Muslim Quarter. I always get up early and by this time of day I often become hungry and had a snack. Walking along through the Muslim Quarter I began to have hungry pangs. As we walked, I saw ahead a street vendor making small breads, much like English muffins but better. I said, "Let's have a snack". Shengwu agreed and insisted on paying for it. They were very inexpensive, costing a few pennies.

As we walked and ate our snack, Shengwu said, "I had never been in this part of Xi'an. I had no idea what was here. You know more about Xi'an than I do."

My feeling was that I might know a few things he did not know but that, in reality, he knew much more than I did.

He began talking about the city. "When the university moved to Xi'an there was not a tree in the city. It was dry, dusty and the people were very poor."

"But the streets are almost all tree-lined now," I said.

"Yes, that is true," he replied, "the university had something like twenty-three train cars loaded with trees come to Xi'an. That is when the trees began to be planted. The first trees were planted at the university. At that time the campus was outside the city at a village. Xi'an ended at the city wall."

Monks practicing their Sanskrit

We continued walking and talking. Finally, we reached the temple complex. Liu Shengwu was surprised at how well it had been maintained. Our visit lasted an hour or so. Finally satisfied with our tour of the temple, we returned to NPU.

Five years later, when Nancy and I worked together editing the papers for the Second International Conference on Project Management I took her to the temple. While walking around the complex we saw several young monks practicing Sanskrit calligraphy. We nodded to each other. Later, as Nancy and I rested on a stone bench, one of the young monks approached us and gave us two peaches which we ate as we rested. We considered this a friendly welcome making this a good visit.

(Note from Nancy-The peaches were tasty, and I felt we had to eat them or insult the monks. This was the first fruit I had ever eaten in China without washing it with soap and water. I suffered from my only case of diarrhea during all my times in China as a result. I would eat the peach again just to be polite as I recovered nicely.)

A Day Trip

Richard

Richard was professor sent from the University of Maryland's campus in Japan to NPU to teach a business methods course for five or six weeks. He was a friendly fellow and we often talked and occasionally ate with others. He loved to brag about the beauty of his Chinese wife. I had to take his word on this as she was not in Xi'an with him.

One day Zhang Qian, from the Foreign Affairs Office asked that the two of us meet her the next day. She would take us downtown and be our tour guide. Richard was happy to go as he had not visited that part of Xi'an and was eager to see the sites. There are too many places to visit in one day but we would do our best.

The next morning, we met her at the appointed time. She smiled and asked, "What would you like to see?"

Richard suggested we go to the Bell Tower, the Foreign Language Bookstore, and the Forest of Steles. I had visited these places before but did not mind going again. We took a taxi to the Bell Tower, getting out on East Street. It was 8:30 a.m. The Bell Tower opened at 9:00 a.m. We had half an hour to window shop.

"Let's go down North Street," I suggested. "I almost never walk on North Street. As we walked, I saw a photography shop where film was developed. "I have film I need to have developed," I said. "Let me leave it here. The sign says it will be ready in an hour." We went into the shop, and I left three rolls of film. The cost was equivalent to $2.00 a roll. I considered this inexpensive.

The Bell Tower

We left the photo shop and walked to the Bell Tower.

Built in 1384 the Bell Tower was considered the center of the universe. Here West, East, North and South streets meet. My friend, Liu Sheng Wu told me that when NPU moved to Xi'an all traffic still ran through the arched tunnels. A traffic circle around the gate was built later to manage the increasing traffic.

We walked back to the Bell Tower, walking through a tunnel that runs under the traffic circle, and past tourist trinkets that were on sale. Zhang bought tickets for us to enter the Bell Tower. Richard said, "I read there are bell concerts several times a day here. The first is at 9:30."

"Let's go to it," Zhang said. "The bells are on the second level. We can look around and be there just before the concert begins."

When we entered the second level, I saw the bells. Counting them I saw there were thirty-nine bells of various sizes in three rows, one above the other. Also, there was a set of thirty pieces of various sized slate, each cut and polished into the shape of an inverted V which. Each slate was hung from the point of the V that pointed upward. There was a woman already in the room playing a many stringed instrument. Soon other musicians came into the room. All were dressed in traditional dress. One man played a bamboo flute, another an Erhu, and a third man struck the large bells. A young woman played the middle and upper row of bells as another young woman played the tuned slates by striking them with drumsticks. The music was pleasant and that surprised me. I had not expected to enjoy the traditional music.

I looked at the construction of the Bell Tower. I saw no nails, and no wooden pegs to hold the Bell Tower together. Rather, the construction looked like Lincoln Log construction. Perhaps this is one reason it has withstood earthquakes over the centuries. Logs such as these could stand rattling around in an earthquake without falling apart.

After the concert ended, we made our way back to the photo shop where I picked up my photographs. Then we made our way along West Street to the Foreign Language bookshop. This was not my first visit, and I knew there was a large selection of well known, inexpensive western books old enough to be out of copyright.

Bill and Zhang Qian

The Bell Tower at night

Recently published western books are very expensive. I was running low on reading material and bought three books.

1. *The Red and Black* by Stendhal
2. *Vanity Fair* by Thackery
3. *Hard Times* by Dicke

Forest of Steles

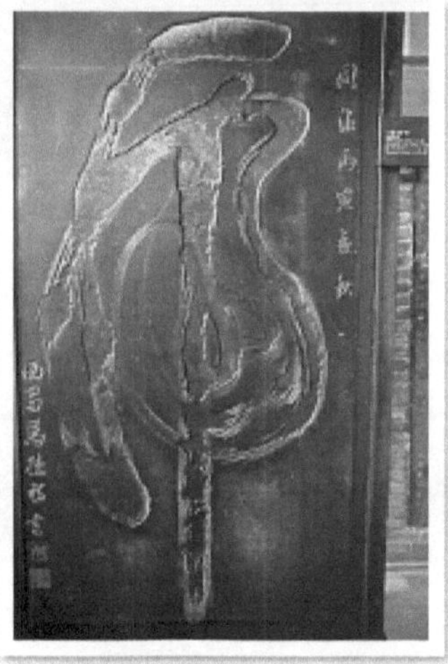

Character for tiger drawn to resemble a tiger

We made our way toward the Northwestern corner of the Ming Wall, the location of the Forest of Steles housed in an ancient Confucian temple. The temple was constructed in the shape of a U with the entrance at the open end. The steles, of which there are over 3,000, are housed in the far end. Porcelain and clay vases, pots and jars are displayed on the two sides of the U. My favorite is a large stele with the character "tiger" carved into it such that the character not only says tiger but resembles a tiger.

Stone hitching posts

Outside the building holding the steles was a collection of stone hitching posts.

We spent over an hour before leaving. Just outside the entrance gate is the ancient Ming wall that surrounds the oldest part of the city.

"Would you like to walk on the wall?" Zhang asked.

Immediately Richard said, "Yes, I'd love to."

Across a narrow street was a set of stairs to the top of the wall. We climbed upward and ambled along the wall to the East Gate in one of the guard houses

Steps to the top of the wall

where ancient weapons were on display. At a second guard house vendors were selling drinks and snack foods. As climbed down to the street level Zhang looked at her watch. "Let's have lunch. It is time."

"Where would you like to eat," I asked. I thought she would mention a good Chinese restaurant and was surprised at her reply.

Zhang laughed, "I love Kentucky Fried Chicken. I want to go there."

"Okay," Richard said. "That is fine with me.

I knew there was a KFC near the South Gate. It was the largest KFC I had seen. A hundred or so people could be seated on the ground floor and over three hundred on the second floor. There were only four cash registers taking orders. This created long lines and waits. They were doing a booming business and had run out of Pepsi Cola. Cokes are never served at KFC.

After lunch we took a taxi back to the university.

On top of the wall

Beggars

Beggars have been with us since the beginning of time. There are 64 verses in the Bible that mention beggars or begging. Beggars appear in literature; Sophocles *Oedipus at Colonus*, Augustine relates a story of passing a beggar in Book VI of his confessions. and there is Magwitch in Dickens *Great Expectations*. Rumi, the great mystic wrote a poem entitled, <u>The Beggar's Courage</u>.

I have been fortunate to have traveled to many countries. There are professional beggars and beggars of opportunity. I saw beggars in most countries; children in Brazil asking for a coin, adults in other countries from the aggressive to beggars on their knees with their foreheads on the pavement between their elbows resting on the cobblestones or concrete. Of course, China, like all countries, also has beggars.

As I wrote this, I was reading the book, *The Girls from St. Petersburg* by Nina Berberova. She wrote the following beggar story:

Ducks were quacking in the dirty slime of the pond. A little girl carrying a baby in her arms opened her mouth wide and dashed after the wagon as fast as she could go.

"Gimme! Gimme! Gimme!"

The doctor whipped the horse on. Now, though, barefoot, bare-assed little boys and girls were running out of every hut and yard, their hands outstretched: "Gimme! Gimme! Gimme!"

Then two older boys, trampling the others, ran after the doctor:

"Sweeties! Sweeties!"[xi]

Mutilated beggar

There was a fast-food restaurant on East Street that I occasionally would go to. It was not a restaurant I had heard of before, not one with an international reputation. However, the food was good and inexpensive. There was always a mutilated beggar outside the restaurant.

He always stood on East Street in the middle of the sidewalk in the oldest part of Xi'an inside the Ming Wall. There always were a few coins and bills lying on a cloth at his feet. Stripped naked to his waist and calling out in a loud voice he could not be missed. When a foreigner walked past, he shouted louder and took a step or two toward them almost blocking their path. Both arms were gone, severed; one almost at the shoulder joint and the other halfway between the elbow and shoulder. Long, large scars crossed his back and chest. My belief was that he was the victim of a terrible industrial accident. I say industrial because of the extent of his now-healed wounds. In Shaanxi Provence in 1995, there were few power tools used in agriculture. Though I asked several people about him, no one knew his story. Everyone had seen him, but no one knew the story of his accident. Someone must have transported him to and from his spot on the street.

The last time I saw him was a wet cold day in October, one of those days when the damp cold penetrates even a wool shirt. There he stood, just as in the heat of summer, no shirt, scars showing, arms missing, calling out to all for a few coins. There is no doubt he was cold. I wondered if he stood there, begging even on the coldest days of winter, shouting, trying to collect a few coins. I also wondered how he got to his place on the sidewalk. Was it by taxi, or did a brother, a sister, or friend help him? I will never know, though I have often wondered.

Five years later in 2000, Nancy and I worked in Xi'an. Early in our stay I purposely went to his spot-on East Street. He was not there nor was the restaurant. I wondered where he was and what had happened to him. I will never know the answer to yet another mystery.

Erhu Beggar

This good-looking young man always sat on West Street, not far from the Bell Tower. Blind, he always sat with his feet in the gutter and his rump on the curb. A brown cloth lay beside him to catch the few coins and bills people dropped. It mattered little whether passersby were in sympathy because of his blindness or in appreciation of his talent. He needed them. Tipping his head upward as if looking into a blue sky he would draw the bow across that beautiful musical instrument, the two strings of his Erhu and beautiful music sprang forth for all to hear. Back and forth, fast and slow the bow glided producing the beautiful *The Butterfly Lover Concerto*. Road traffic receded as the music rose. This young blind man, just out of childhood, played as if pouring his soul into the music. I like to think that he was 'discovered' and became known and has lived a comfortable life. I fear he has remained a blind beggar, sitting on a dusty sidewalk, in the heat of summer and cold of winter, playing for a few coins. My heart filled with sadness as I dropped a bill onto his cloth. Then I made my way through the Drum Tower into the Muslim Quarter of Xi'an.

Peasant Beggar

On his elbows and knees, his forehead resting on the sidewalk, his hands stretched in front of his head, palms up. He was begging. "Strange," I thought. "His clothes aren't torn and tattered. In fact, they look rather new, clean and there are no patches."

Later back at NPU I described what I had seen to a friend. "Oh," they replied, "he wasn't a beggar, not in the true sense of the word. No, he was a peasant who came to Xi'an on a day off. He begs simply hoping to fool a few people and get a bit of money. Tomorrow he will be back in the fields working with other peasants."

I remembered that while visiting friends in Hefei that Lao Wang had refused to give any coins to a beggar for the same reason. "He is not a beggar; his clothes are too good" Wang had said. "He is a peasant in town for the day and hopes to collect some money. I will never give to such people.

Playing Pool in Xi'an

John and Mike Carroll

I walked out of my room in the guesthouse and down the steps to the ground floor. I saw a man and a teenage boy checking into the guesthouse. I knew at once they were either American or Canadian. I stopped and waited for them to finish their registration. Then I stepped forward and introduced myself.

The man shook my hand and said, "I am John Carroll, and this is my son Mike."

"Are you going to be here for several days?" I knew that professors from various universities in the West come and give lectures at NPU.

"Yes," he said. "I'm going to give several lectures over the next few days."

"Do you have any plans for this evening, anything you would like to do? I was just getting ready to go to supper."

"No, we have no plans. Do you have a suggestion close by?"

"I could take you down to the Bell Tower and show you around the old part of the city. We could have a good meal of Chinese dumplings."

The professor and his son smiled. "That would be great we have been wanting to eat Chinese dumplings, Jiaozi, since we arrived in Beijing. But we couldn't find any there."

"OK. Wait a minute. I want to call someone and see if she can go with us. She has lived in Xi'an several years and knows the city better than I."

I called Ruth, an American lady who lived with her husband on the NPU campus. She agreed that she would go along.

Ruth joined us. We walked out of the South gate of the university and caught a taxi. The driver took an unusual route which turned out to be a mistake. He drove toward the Xi'an sports arena. As luck would have it there was something going on there that night and it looked like all four million people who lived in the inner city were there or trying to get in. There was a tangle of cars, motorcycles, bicycles, and walkers. Even the walkers were just creeping along because the crowd was so thick. Finally, the driver got through the gridlock and let us out at the South gate of the Ming wall. We walked down South Street to the Bell Tower And then onto East Street and the jiaozi restaurant. Upon entering the restaurant, we told the waitress that we wanted jiaozi for four people. We were quite surprised. They swore on a stack of Deng Xiaoping's writings that they had sold all their jiaozi that day.

Suddenly Ruth spoke up. "I know a little restaurant on North Street. I have eaten there and their jiaozi is good."

I was glad I had invited Ruth to go with us as I would have been lost and had no way of finding another jiaozi restaurant in that part of the city. I knew where we could have gotten baozi and where a good Muslim restaurant was, but not jiaozi.

The restaurant was excellent, one a tourist never visited. I believe every employee and the owner's daughter came in to look at we foreigners.

After eating, we caught a taxi to return to the university. This time the taxi went down West Street, through the huge West Gate through the Ming dynasty wall and on to NPU. We got out on the little side street that led to the East Gate of the university. Walking along the street we passed pool tables that sat on the side of the street. Through summer, winter, spring, and fall, through snow, sleet, hail, rain, heat and cold the tables sit there. John and Mike said they wanted to play a game of pool. There was one table empty, and we paid the owner 1 kwai, 1 Chinese dollar. He racked the balls up and we began to play. Soon a huge crowd of Chinese crowded around the table to watch the foreigners play.

None of us were particularly good and on these tables we really were bad. A pool table is supposed to be flat. This table was anything but flat. Sitting outside year-round in rain, sleet, snow, heat, and cold had warped them. There was a hill here and a valley there and random rips in the green felt cloth. When we hit the cue ball or when another ball was hit, we never knew where it was really going to go. It was a guessing game watching the ball roll, twist and turn. One shot slowly rolled across the table toward a ball that the shooter hoped would go into a corner pocket. The cue ball slowly approached and suddenly rolled left then straight and then right coming to rest directly behind the ball he had hoped to hit. We all had a good laugh.

After the great pool shootout, we walked on to the university and called it a day.

D is for Dragonfly

The day was a typical Xi'an summer day, hot, dry, and dusty. The sun shone through the Gobi Desert dust that always fills the sky. Midafternoon Qian Fupei came to my room. I was working, as usual, sitting on the end of the bed with the computer on the sideboard that stood against the wall.

"How is it going?" he asked.

"Good," I replied.

"I want you to eat with Yeying and me this evening. I will come for you at 5:00. OK?"

"Yes," I replied. "That will be fine.

Fupei left, returning to his office. At five that evening he knocked on the door and entered. "Are you ready?"

"Yes," I said.

He turned opening the door. "I will stop at the corner store and buy a loaf of bread. We need it for our evening meal."

We left my room and made our way to the corner store. Entering we walked to where the bread was on the shelf. Fupei picked up a loaf, squeezed it and put it back on the shelf. He picked up a second load and repeated the process. Then a third, a fourth, a fifth time. Each time he squeezed the loaf and replaced it on the shelf.

I was amazed. "They are all the same," I thought. "Each is just like the other. He just can't make up his mind." I was becoming exasperated, standing, and waiting. Finally, he picked up a loaf, turned and paid for it.

"Let's go," he said.

We walked on to his apartment. Yeying was cooking when we arrived. When everything was ready, we sat at a round table on their balcony. As we ate, I happened to look out toward the building across the alleyway. I could not believe my eyes.

"Look", I said. "Look there are thousands of dragonflies flying slowly to the West."

Fupei and Yeying gasped. "I've never seen that before!" Fupei said.

We stood watching for five or ten minutes. The dragonflies continued to pass, slowly flying westward.

I did not know at that time that dragonflies migrate. Where these came from and where they were going, I have no idea. Xi'an is in a semi-arid part of the country and there is little water nearby.

I have unsuccessfully searched the Internet trying to gain insight into this phenomenon but have found nothing about dragonfly migration in Shaanxi Province.

T Is for Tooth

I stood in front of the mirror brushing my teeth. "Hmmm," I thought, "something feels funny with my front tooth. The last time I had this feeling ... "oh God, a root canal!" I opened my mouth and gingerly touched the tooth. It wiggled! "Ah shucks," I groaned to myself, "here I am half a world away from home and my crown has come unglued. I'm not only half a world away, but I have four months to go before I return home.

Cautiously I rocked the tooth back and forth again hoping a miracle had occurred and the tooth would be firm. The tooth rocked back and forth freely. No miracle. I decided to give the tooth one more test. I gently pulled on the crown. To my dismay. It offered no resistance but slid out. With a steadily sinking feeling in the pit of my stomach I stood staring at the crown, now clutched in my fingers. I turned on the water in the sink. Just as I was about to place the crown under the running water my mind screamed, "Stop, you don't want Mao's revenge. Wash it in boiled water, stupid." Walking back into my little bedroom, I washed the crown with boiled water from my thermos.

I pushed the crown back in place and sat down on my bed to think. I had a small tube of Fix-o-dent in my suitcase, a gag gift at my retirement party, which I decided to bring to China as a last-minute thing while packing. Could I live with a Fix-o-dent crown for four months? I really did not want to find out, but it appeared this was now a distinct possibility.

I knew what a dentist needed to do to secure the crown in place. I was an old hand at this experience. The question was, "Is there a dentist in Xi'an with the epoxy, the knowledge and skill to reattach the crown?"

Gloomily, I sat thinking. "In a city of four million people there must be such a dentist. How do I find this dentist?" Three years before I had seen a sidewalk dentist with a foot powered drill. If my choice was between Fix-o-dent and a sidewalk dentist, well, that would be an easy decision. I decided my best course of action was to go to the university Foreign Affairs Office in the morning and ask for their help. It is at times like this that my mind goes into overdrive. What if I swallow the crown while I am asleep? Should I leave the crown in or out? What is the chance of infection? Dozens of questions swirled around and around in my mind, questions for which I had no good answers.

The next morning, I walked to the Foreign Affairs Office. Zhang Qian was the only person in the office when I arrived at nine o'clock. Already the temperature was above 90 degrees and climbing rapidly. Perhaps there was a correlation between my anxiety and the day's heat.

"How are you this morning?" Zhang Qian said smiling.

"I have a problem and need your help." I spoke with a confidence I did not feel.

The smile disappeared from Zhang's face. "What's wrong?"

I told her about my tooth ending with, "Do you know any dentist in Xi'an where I can have the cap reglued?"

She thought for a moment, "Let me call the university hospital," she said. "I'll see if they can help or tell us who can. If they can't help, I'll call my husband. He is a doctor.

We walked across the hallway to the department phone just outside of the director's office. Picking up the phone, she dialed the hospital. After a few moments, I heard a rapid-fire conversation. My Chinese was much too poor to follow the discussion. After about five minutes Zhang Qian hung up the phone. Turning to me she said, "Come back at two this afternoon. I'll go to the hospital with you. They can do the work for you."

"That's great!" I said relieved, "I thought I would have to go to one of the big hospitals downtown."

"No," she replied, "no trips downtown. By the way, don't meet me here. I'll meet you in front of my apartment building. My apartment is in Building One, it is close to the hospital."

At two o'clock, we walked out of the blazing heat into the cool of the hospital. The coolness surprised me as the hospital was not air-conditioned. Entering the dentist's office, I noticed there was no reception area. Four dentist chairs stood side-by-side, facing the windows. Overhead a Casablanca-type paddle-wheel fan turned slowly. All the windows were open creating good cross ventilation.

"Oh my God," I thought, "they still use belt driven drills." The sight of these took me back to my childhood. When I was a child, nothing struck terror in my heart like the sight of slow-speed belt driven drills. They not only hurt, but made my head vibrate as the dentist drilled on a tooth.

Dust, an inch thick, lay in the spittoon and over an unused chair. It was not that there was an unused or broken chair that bothered me. Rather it was that it was dirty. It had been years since being cleaned, or so it appeared to me. Cleanliness and sanitation were not a high priority. This did nothing to lessen a small nagging fear in my mind concerning picking up an infection or making a quantum leap to the big league, AIDS.

A dentist and her assistant were working on a young man sitting in the second chair. We had arrived too late for me to figure out what they were doing to their patients. I was encouraged in that he was not moaning and groaning. Several familiar dental tools lay on the dentist's working tray. It seemed they were in the final stages of work on this patient.

Zhang Qian began an animated conversation with the dentist. I didn't have to be a linguist to realize I was the object of their conversation. The young man in the chair joined the conversation, when the dentist was not working on his teeth. I was rather amused realizing that I was giving several people a topic of conversation to discuss over the evening's meal.

"Has she worked on foreigners before?" I asked.

A short conversation followed. Zhang Qian turned to me, "Yes, but not often. Sometimes foreign teachers need to see a dentist and she has helped them."

I wandered around the room looking at the equipment and watching the dentist. Various dental tools lay on the counter behind the chairs. I could see no difference between those the tools lying here and those used in the States. I did not see a sterilizer. This gave me an uncomfortable feeling. However, I couldn't bring myself to believe that tools were not sterilized between use on one patient and the next. I was glad that I had taken Hepatitis B shots before leaving home.

During this time several other people came into the room, joined the conversation, looked both the dentist's patient and me over and then left. After about ten minutes the young man got out of the chair and left. It was now my turn!

With a smile the dental assistant motioned for me to sit in the chair. After clipping a bib to my shirt, she motioned for me to open my mouth. Opening my mouth, I wiggled the crown for the assistant and the dentist. The dentist picked up a pair of tweezers and with a deft motion folded some cotton around them. Taking the cotton with her fingers she carefully removed the crown and held it up for all to see.

Carrying the crown, she walked out of sight behind me. Suddenly, I heard the whine of a high-speed drill. My thought was, "I wonder where she hides the high-speed drill." I had not noticed such a drill. It was not part of the chair. How did she get the drill and the patient together?

As the dentist cleaned the tooth her assistant pulled a swab from a roll of cotton and soaked it with an antiseptic. A familiar smell brought memories from my childhood. I also remembered the taste, but I could not remember the name of the antiseptic.

The dentist, having finished cleaning the crown, now picked up a mental tool and began cleaning the old glue from what was left of my real tooth. She then selected what looked like a drill bit the size of a needle and inserted it into the empty root canal. Removing the needle like drill bit she checked it said one word which sounded like the Chinese equivalent of "Yuck." Then she showed it to her assistant. She repeated this procedure several times. Finally, she laid it on a tray and said, "Clean." This was the only word she said in English during my visit.

Lastly, I heard the assistant mixing something behind me. I knew the sound of epoxy being mixed. Carefully she inserted the cap back in place. Showing me with facial expressions what she wanted me to do she checked the bite. She was no wimp in conducting this procedure. She didn't, like my American dentist, use carbon paper to check the bite. Rather, she inserted the crown and leaned close to eyeball my bite. After two manipulations of the crown, she nodded her head in satisfaction. The bite was right.

I got up from the chair feeling pleased. I was impressed by the care the dentist showed throughout the procedure. I'd assumed she would simply re-glue the crown.

"Wait a minute," Zhang Qian said. "I want the dentist to check me." Zhang Qian sat in the chair I had just vacated. While waiting for Zhang Qian I saw the high-speed drill. Much to my surprise it was a mobile high-speed drill. The drill apparatus was a self-contained unit. All that was necessary was to fill the water tank with boiled water, plug in the electrical cord, attach a drill bit and the dentist would be ready for action. Having never conceived of a drill being mobile I stood there amazed. This reminded me of electronic instruments I have seen in auto repair shops. I wondered how dentists speak to each other when working. "Hey buddy, roll the drill over here, I've got one to work on."

Cultural Revolution – 1966-1976

The Cultural Revolution was a time of chaos, murder, mayhem, destruction, and disaster in China. I was told that on the NPU Campus there was a civil war between factions, each claiming to be the true followers and supporters of Mao Zedong. Every person still alive from that era has stories of that tragic time. I know only a few of those stories.

V is for Victim

I was walking down Scholar Street to the "Corner Store" the first time I saw him. Walking toward me, body bent forward, cigarette dangling from his lips, he shuffled along the sidewalk. I noticed his blue Mao jacket and trousers were in sharp contrast with his white shirt. I had seen such trousers often on a trip to China in 1986. Everyone, men, women, even children wore Mao trousers. In 1995, a few peasant men wore Mao trousers and jackets, but I had not seen any city dweller wearing these clothes of that past era. Perhaps the peasants wore them only because they discarded nothing until it was torn and in tatters. But this was a city dweller. A battered straw hat sat on his head, sweat stains showed on the multi-colored band. A slight Mona Lisa smile played on his mouth. His eyes twinkled. He clasped his hands together in front as he walked. There was something about this man, something about his walk, the tilt of his body, the gleam in his eye, the smile on his face that said, "All is not well with this man." He nodded as we passed but said nothing.

"Strange," I thought, "I haven't seen him before. I wonder what he is doing here, on campus. What is his story?"

I continued walking on to the Corner Store where I bought a bottle of Jin-Mei-La, a Chinese soft drink[xii] and sat down an outdoor table. Sitting in the shade, I sipped my soft drink thinking about the man I had just seen.

For each person, there is a story. I had a feeling this man's story was not a happy one. China is a land full of stories that no one will hear. Fear is the inhibitor, especially within the older generation. Every family has members or friends who suffered for uttering politically incorrect words, both spoken or written, during the Great Proletarian Cultural Revolution. During my six months in China, I suggested to friends that they write their memoirs as they had lived in interesting and historic times. The almost universal answer was, "I would like to, but I am afraid to do so."

Often, as I walked near the Corner Store, I would see this man shuffling along. He always was dressed in white shirt and blue Mao trousers and a jacket with a straw hat sitting at an angle on his head. Occasionally he carried a liter bottle of beer. A cigarette always dangled from his lips.

Ruth

One hot July evening I was eating a dish of noodles at the *Happy Lady's Restaurant*. I had joined two other "foreign American devils," Ruth and Richard for supper. Richard was teaching a short course dealing with some aspect of American business methods. He loved to brag about his beautiful Chinese wife.

Ruth had taught English in Xi'an for four years She had made the poor decision of marrying a Chinese professor. She expected a nice American husband, and he expected a nice Chinese wife. Both were disappointed and were in divorce proceedings.

"Ruth", I said, "I've noticed a man walking around the campus who seems to be sort of 'out of it.' He looks harmless enough but there really is something wrong."

Ruth took a drink from her ever-present beer. "Tell me about him. I think I know who you mean."

"Well," I said, "I've seen him several times walking around the campus. He's almost always near the Corner Store. He wears a straw hat, a white shirt, and blue Mao trousers probably from an old Mao suit. He holds his hands in front of him and walks along with a strange little smile on his face."

"Oh, yeah, I know him," she exclaimed! "He's a very friendly guy; one of the crazies who roam about the campus. God, his is a tragic story. Occasionally I buy him a beer. There are several women on campus who are crazies also, but I don't know much about them."

"Tell me about him."

Ruth took another swig of beer and thought for several moments before beginning. With a sigh, she began. "His tragedy is one of the many that happened here during the Cultural Revolution. It's the same with the women, I guess. Christ, it's the same all over China. Anyway, before the Cultural Revolution, he was the head of one of the maintenance work units on campus. People told me that he was very fair and good to people in his work unit, a good boss. He was married, had a son ... life was good; about as good as it could be in those times. He had a job, a family and didn't have to worry about his basic needs. He didn't have much, but then no one had much. Poverty was evenly spread among the populace. No one except the top dogs were rich. Then the Cultural Revolution came along."

Ruth paused wiping the sweat from her face. She tipped her bottle away and stared at its contents.

"What happened?" I asked. "I know there was a little civil war between the various factions on campus; that people were killed, driven to suicide, and some were murdered."

"That's true," she replied. Then with a sigh, she repeated, "the Cultural Revolution came along. The campus split into factions. Everyone was the 'true' supporter of Mao. God, it makes me sick. I don't know which group he was a part of, or if he was a part of any group. He probably was part of some group; too damned dangerous not to be and damned dangerous if you were. I'm told it was total chaos."

"Yeah," I replied, "I've heard the same thing."

"Anyway, someone accused him of being a Capitalist Roader[xiii] or some such nonsense. Anyone could accuse anyone of almost anything and God help you 'cause you were guilty when accused. So, he was accused and in big trouble. The Red Guards and others picked on him, hounded him and put him on public display, you know, the dunce cap, the sign ... there were the usual struggle sessions where he was forced to kneel and take the 'airplane position.' "

Those who were detained often faced beatings, and they were pulled along with their heads forced down and their hands twisted up behind, a modified version of the "airplane position" that was a standard method of abuse during the Cultural Revolution.[xiv]

Richard cut in, "What the hell is the airplane position?"

"Damned if I know," she replied laughing. "I don't know why, but I've never asked. Maybe I'm afraid someone would tell me."

I laid my chopsticks on my plate before answering. "That I do know," I said. "It was when they forced the person to lean forward as far as possible. They had to hold their hands behind their back and raise them as far as possible. Usually, they were forced to kneel on a small board or something uncomfortable. If you lowered your arms, they'd beat and kick you until you resumed the airplane position. I was told about a woman who actually went to sleep in this position while being struggled against."

"You're kidding!" Ruth snorted. "I can't believe that!"

"Honest," I said, "that's what I was told. She was struggled against so often, was so tired that she actually went to sleep and stayed in the airplane position. The Red Guards went bananas when they realized she had gone to sleep. Proof positive she was an 'enemy of the people.' "

"How long would they have to hold that position?" Richard asked with an incredulous look. "I saw some bad stuff, like people starving to death, when I was here in 1946, but nothing like that."

"Sometimes for hours" I replied. "Mercy was not a virtue."

"Damn," Ruth said as she took a long drink, "that's terrible, but I believe it. Anyway, he, his wife and small son went through a hell of a rough time. Finally, whoever was in charge decided to send them to the countryside for re-education. You know, 'learn from the peasants.' Someone told him the Red Guards were coming to get him. He ran to his apartment and hid under the bed. But they found him. Hell isn't that the first place to look!"

"Is that when his mind snapped?" I asked.

"No, worse was to come. When he was forced to watch the murder of his son his mind snapped. Murdered is the only word for it. I don't know the details only that it was not a quick death. Guess someone changed their mind about sending the kid to the countryside. They forced him to watch as they abused and struggled against his wife. I've been afraid to ask what they did to her. I don't want to know. He became like a sailor guiding his craft on a sea with no shore, no starts to navigate by, and a sea with no ports of call."

"Both were sent to the countryside. He's never seen or heard anything about his wife since. He's been off in his own little world."

"God, after all that, did they really send him to the countryside?" Richard looked like he was about to throw up.

"Sure did. Don't know how long he was stuck in the boonies. They finally let him come back to the university ... not that it did much good. He couldn't work anymore. Can't really do anything for himself except eat, drink a beer, and smoke a cigarette. He just wanders around the campus with that little smile on his face."

Ruth waved her empty bottle over her head. This was her way of ordering another beer.

"Whenever I see him," Ruth continued, "I talk with him for a minute or two. Sometimes I'll buy him a beer or a pack of cigarettes. Poor devil, I feel sorry for him. You'll never see anyone on campus talking to him. The only people I've ever seen talking with him are us ', foreign devils.' I guess people are embarrassed to be seen talking with him. Maybe it brings back too many of their own bitter memories."

We all sat in silence, each with our own thoughts. Silently I wondered, "How would I have handled that? Not as well as he. Who can blame him for snapping, losing it and retreating into his own world? Not me!" I sat staring at my Chinese soft drink and plate of noodles. I wasn't very hungry now. I don't know how long I sat thinking.

Setting his chopsticks down Richard spoke, "How does he take care of himself? You say he's in his own world."

"Oh," Ruth aid between sips of beer, "the university gives him a room to live in. Someone cooks for him and takes care of his clothes. I don't know, maybe a relative. The university seems to treat him well enough. Maybe it helps soothe their guilty conscience, the bastards. Well, hell, at least he seems to be happy in his world." Ruth took a long swig from her beer and wiped her eye, "That's more than I can say for most people ... including myself," she whispered.

Comfort Woman

Just then an elderly woman shuffled past. Ruth pointed at her and said, "See that woman? Her story is tragic also. Caught by the Japanese they made her one of their 'comfort women'.[xv] God only knows how many tragic stories there are on this campus … or any Chinese campus or in any family.

Often during the remaining months of my stay, I saw that man. His dress stayed the same through the long hot summer. The Mona Lisa smile never left his face. He shuffled along in his own world, in his own time, in his own place; a world, a time and a place I could never visit.

The last time I saw him was on a cold, rainy day in October a blue Mao jacket covered his white shirt. I watched as he shuffled along, beer in hand, cigarette hanging from his smiling mouth. "What world are you in?" "What do you remember?" "Do you feel the pain that is still deep within you?" I'll never know.

Nancy and I returned to NPU in 2000. I was there for six months and Nancy for ten. I do not know what happened to this man, we never saw him.

P is for Pigs

I was talking with one of my friends, Yu, and the topic of the Cultural Revolution came up.

"Were you struggled against," I asked.

"Yes," she replied, "I was, but not as much as others."

"Were you sent to the countryside?" I had another friend who had been sent far into the countryside to a peasant village.

"Not at first," Yu replied. "The Red Guards gave me the job of taking care of the pigs?"

"Pigs?"

"Yes, at that time we raised pigs on the campus. The Red Guards thought this was a nasty, bad job when they gave it to me. What they did not know, and I did not tell them was I enjoyed the job. I liked taking care of the pigs. If they had known I liked the job, they would have given me another nasty job, like cleaning toilets. I just kept my mouth shut." She laughed. "I was clever, and they never knew."

"How many pigs did you care for?" I found this a very interesting conversation.

Smiling she replied, "About forty. The university raised them to help supply meat to the workers. I took care of my pigs for several years. Then they sent me to Eastern Shaanxi, to the countryside,"

"What did you do there?"

"Oh, the village gave me the job of raising vegetables. That was a good job also. I was lucky and survived with few problems. Others were not as lucky.

C is for Cook

Another friend, Qian, told me about his experience during the Cultural Revolution.

"I was too old to be a Red Guard and too young to be a big enemy of the people. I tried to stay out of the way by going to the library every day and reading."

"Were you sent to the countryside?"

"Yes," he replied, "time passed, and I was sent to the countryside. They took me by train and then by truck as far as the truck could go. Peasants met us and led me to their village. It was a long walk and often on a narrow path with long drops on one side."

"Were you given a job?" I wondered what type of work he was given. Life in a remote village is difficult.

"The peasants were good people," he said. "They realized that if I had to work as hard as they that it would kill me. So, they gave me the job of being the village assistant cook."

"That is interesting," I said. "What did you cook?"

"My job was to grind corn, not cook. The corn was boiled and that is what we ate every day, every meal. There was nothing else."

"No meat?" I inquired.

"No," he said, "a pig was too valuable to eat. They might sell a pig and use the money to buy something the village needed, like a new hoe or take. They would never eat a pig."

"You have respect for the peasants? I asked. I have heard some Chinese speaking insulting remarks about peasants.

"Oh, yes, I respect them a lot. They have a hard life and yet they treated me well. Since living there and eating only boiled ground corn I realize that everything that I eat is good."

Expats Restaurants

Lori and Zhou Liping on way to eat at The Boss

After the first few weeks in Xi'an, I seldom ate my lunch or evening meal at the university restaurant. It was neither that the food was bad nor was it that the food was expensive. In fact, I could eat there free. The problem was it was the same over and over and over and this became quite tiring. It's not much fun eating by yourself and eating the same food over and over is boring.

There were four restaurants our group of friends frequented almost exclusively. Of these four we ate at two almost all the time. One the ex-pats had tagged the first "The Happy Lady's" and the other we tagged "The Boss." I have no idea what the real name of either restaurant was, and I am not sure I ever knew. Both were near the university. The third restaurant, we seldom frequented was tagged, "The Bitch".

The fourth restaurant was across the street from the south gate of the university. I never knew its name and we never gave it a nickname. It was more expensive, and we seldom ate there.

Each day four to six of us, a combination of ex-pats and Chinese would make our way to one of these restaurants to eat. The food was so inexpensive we ex-pats almost always paid for our Chinese friend's meals. At that time, I could eat two substantial meals for about a dollar a day.

These restaurants had become popular because as one ex-pat said, "We have never gotten Mao's revenge at these restaurants.

The Boss

"The Boss Restaurant" was on a narrow street filled with small shops and restaurants. This is no longer true. Using Google Earth, I can now see those tall buildings line the street.

We would go to "The Boss" in the evening and always ordered his delicious jiaozi, Chinese dumplings. That one dish was his entire menu and that was all the menu he needed. His jiaozi were delicious.

The boss himself was middle aged, taller, and more muscular than most Chinese. He had six or seven tables sitting on the sidewalk where we would eat. He also had a few inside tables, but we avoided these as it was smoky inside and we could not watch life on the street from inside.

He knew us and when he would see us walking down the crowded street, he would grab a table and drag it to a 'good shady spot,' and as we sat, he would ask by holding up fingers asking, "How many?" The question was not how many people, but how many plates of jiaozi. The next question was how many beers and how many Cokes. Water was totally out of the question. Water was a sure way to catch a dreadful digestive upset.

We tagged him "The Boss" for several reasons. He never cooked. He never served the plates. He did circulate among the customers, especially the expats. But most of all he earned the name from the way he would stand on the third step up from the street, hands folded across his chest as he surveyed the street and his customers. He had the look of a man who knew how to take care of himself and thus how to take care of his customers if anyone bothered them. He was the boss.

Happy Lady's Restaurant

We called her the Happy Lady as she was always friendly and in a happy mood. Her restaurant had two tables under a woven plastic awning. Her stove was a cutoff 50-gallon drum lined with baked-on loess mud with a large wok sitting on the top. One meal was cooked at a time. There was no printed menu. To order we would tell her what we wanted, and it would appear. It was always good.

Walking to the Happy Lady Restaurant

I open the door to my room and step into the hallway. The dusty carpet is soft under my feet. To my right, two doors away are large double doors that lead to a banquet room. I turn left, ahead of me, at the far end of the hallway, I see the black hair of the young woman on duty. Her job is to watch the hallway and refill thermos bottles with boiling water. This surely is a boring job. Just the top of her head shows above the counter. She is either daydreaming or sleeping. I smile to myself thinking, Nap time ended at 2:30 p.m. "At 5:00 p.m. she is probably reading, or perhaps she is ignoring me, fearing I will speak English to her. None of the 'hall girls' show interest in speaking to me.

I turn right at the head of the stairs and walk down two flights of stairs to the lobby. I check the brightly colored fly paper hanging at the window to see how many flies are stuck to the glue. The paper is quite full. I avoid the loose metal strip near the bottom of the stairs. It has been loose for two months. Three weeks ago, I showed the manager the problem, but nothing has changed. Apparently, he does not consider it worthy of attention. I am continually surprised that no one has tripped or fallen. I chuckled thinking that OSHA would have a field day here.

At the bottom of the steps, to the right, two young women are sitting behind the registration desk. A young maintenance man is leaning on the desk, flirting with them. I hear low voices and giggles as I pass. None pay any attention to me. Romance, real or imagined or simple teasing is more interesting than a white-headed foreigner. On the opposite wall, a digital clock shows the time and date in large letters and larger numbers. The clock and my growling stomach tell me it is time to eat.

I walk across the lobby. On the wall to my left are four clocks showing the time in Beijing, Tokyo, London, and New York. I notice the New York clock is still on standard time, not daylight savings. I realize that everyone 'back home' is asleep.

I push the glass door open and step out into the covered driveway made of yellow, black, and white stone. The yellow stones look like they have been dyed. The dry heat of the day strikes me, almost taking my breath away. I put on my Aussie hat and stepped into the sunshine. I feel my shirt absorbing the heat. The coolness I felt in my air-conditioned room quickly dissipates. My skin turns hot. Sweat evaporates so quickly my shirt stays dry.

I turn left and walk down the inclined driveway and across to one of the gates. A rod iron fence with two gates surrounds the hotel. Tall shrubs grow on the inside of the fence casting shade into the hotel yard. Crepe Myrtle is interspersed along the fence. It is in full bloom, with a variety of red and white blossoms. Now I must walk in the full sun, in the full heat of the sun.

A layer of yellow dust covers the driveway, the fence, the leaves as well as the street. Wind continually blows yellow dust from the Gobi Desert and the fine dust covers everything both inside and out. There is no escape. Living here and breathing the air is like smoking a pack or two of cigarettes each day. Also, there is unseen industrial air pollution. Maybe I should adjust the smoking to three packs a day. I walk, hoping the wind will lie quietly at rest. Wind often has brought dust to my eyes, nose, and throat, to say nothing about my hair and clothing. Today I am fortunate, as there is not a whisper of a breeze.

I pass through the gate and turn left onto the intersecting street. Students on bicycles and walking pass in every direction. A young couple passes on two bicycles. They ride side by side, his arm around her waist. I watch their feet rising and falling as they peddle. Ah, young and in love; romance on a bicycle?

I walk close to the fence trying not to obstruct the bicycles. I can see the patterns of the tire tracks in the dust, even on concrete. I walk on and turn left at the first intersection. To my right is a small building with a tiny store in one corner. Two round tables with two chairs each sit outside in the blazing sun. A soft drink machine stands at the corner of the building. Beside the store is a small kitchen serving food to students. A bowl filled with nondescript food sits on the table. I look at the food and say to myself, "I think I will pass on this." As they serve students, I am not sure they can sell me food as I am neither a student nor a professor.

I stop and watch as students walk up to the table with their own small porcelain bowls to be filled. It is not considered an insult to a restaurant to carry your own bowl and chopsticks and to use them instead of the restaurant's dishes and chopsticks. Deftly, she takes the bowl, fills it with food and hands it back to the student. Few students are eating here. It is too hot and there is no shade, and the stools are in full sunshine. With their bowls filled, they turn and return to their dorm to eat. Most walk-in twos and threes, talking, laughing, nibbling at their food. Others walk alone silently. I see one student, bowl in hand, head down as if in deep thought, walking slowly toward the dorm. I am curious about what deep thoughts he is thinking. Is it a personal problem or an academic problem?

I walk on and carefully step over water running across the concrete. The water comes from the guest house restaurant kitchen and gives off the smell of dirty dishwater. It drains directly from a sink onto the concrete and then onto the ground. Every time I pass this way, there is smelly running water to step over. I am always a little disgusted as I skirt the mud and step over the water. Then I carefully step over an open manhole into which the dirty water drains. The manhole cover, overgrown with grass, lays nearby. "Why has no one put it back in place. Doesn't anyone care about safety?" I wonder if China has liability laws. Years later in 2000, I was told by a university official that there are no liability laws in China.

Deep, cool shade from rows of Cottonwood trees beacons just ahead. I quicken my pace and enjoy the coolness of the shade as it engulfs my body. Blessed shade on a hot day.

To my left is a five-story graduate student dormitory where five or six graduate students live in each room. Bicycles are parked in front of the building. Students sit on the shaded front steps, eating, talking, and laughing. Drying laundry hangs out the windows on sticks attached to the wall. The laundry is a dead giveaway as to which gender lives in that room.

Ahead of me are old brown stucco one-room apartment buildings. Young professors live here. When I visited my friend, Xiao Ou, I saw that his room measures about 9 by 15 feet. There is no privacy here for him, his wife, or his son. I assume children learn the 'facts of life' early. I turn right as I near the apartments and walk beside them.

To my right is a bicycle parking building. An attendant sits on an old wooden chair placed in the doorway. The attendant, a woman, watches the world go by and only allows those with bicycles to enter the building. Hundreds of bicycles are parked inside. Bicycle theft is prevalent and a constant problem.

I walk along. Little kids squat as they play in the dust. I can see their little bottoms showing through the split-bottom pants.

Clothing for toddlers in China is interesting. There is a split in the seams at the crotch. When nature calls they squat, the seam opens allowing them to 'go to the toilet' on the ground without soiling their clothes. It doesn't matter if it is number 1 or number 2, on to the ground it goes. Grandmothers sweep up number 2 into paper bags. One other aspect of the split seam gives me pause.

When the kids sat down the seam opens and they sit bare butt on the ground, in the dust.

Some are totally naked except for an apron covering their chest and belly button. They sit, bare bottomed in the dust. I wonder how many kids, especially little girls, have bladder infections from sitting and playing in the dust. The cool earth must feel good to a bare bottom. The mothers and grandmothers sit and gossip as they watch these little ones.

I turn left and walk between two apartment buildings. Just past the buildings, I step over a deep, concrete-lined drainage ditch on the side of a wide street running to the East gate. Now the young professor's apartments are to my right. To my left is a chain link fence. Beyond the fence is a row of six pool tables, all fully occupied by students. Beyond the pool tables are four basketball courts. Eight half-court games are in full swing. I see sweat glistening on the young men as they play. Groups of young women stand, watching the players. They never join one of the games. They stand, watch and whisper to each other. Are we not all, or almost all, interested in the opposite sex at this age? I smile to myself, wondering how aware the male players are of the young women watching. Surely, they are aware.

I approach the East Gate and walk between large metal bars placed to prevent automobiles and trucks from entering or leaving the university. Walkers, bicycles, and motorbikes squeeze through. A guard sits outside a small guardhouse, watching everyone leaving or entering. "Another boring job," I think, "but it is a job. So many are unemployed in China." The government claims there is no unemployment, just youth waiting for work. My feeling is that a rose by any other name is still unemployment.

Fruit and vegetables for sale

I step through the gate back into the hot sun leaving the world of the university and into what at first appears to be chaos. I turn left once through the gate. On my left, the street is lined with small shops and tiny restaurants. Almost all are restaurants with tables and chairs under plastic tarps. Three-sided cinder block cubicles butt against the university wall. I feel the heat from a large griddle where little round breads are cooked. They are somewhat like English muffins. However, the consistency is much heavier. Smoke rises from the charcoal fires that heat the woks.

Grains and dried vegetables

Flames shoot two to three feet upward as rape seed oil vaporizes off the red-hot surfaces. Steaming plates of food are being devoured by hungry customers. It is as if each restaurant is a duplicate of the others. Peasant tricycle cabs line the opposite side of the street. Fish, pork, beef, noodles, watermelon, bananas, grapes, Chinese cabbage, eggplants, potatoes, onions carrots, hundred-pound bags of spices and dried beans, peas, and a host of other fruits and vegetables are for sale. On streets in the summer corn was cooked, in the fall chestnuts were roasted, and in winter sweet potatoes were roasted. The corn was field corn, not sweet corn which to my tastebuds left much to be desired.

I see a peasant weighting carrots for a woman. The summer sun has darkened his skin to a deep mahogany. His muscles ripple as he lifts the carrots and places them in a metal container at the end of a hand-held scale. The scale is made of a long stick with notches at regular intervals. A pear-shaped plum bob is attached to the far end of the metal pan. He slides the plum bob along the stick until the scale balances. Holding the scale-up he shows the woman the weight. Quickly he dumps the carrots into the bag she opens. Carefully she counts her money and places it in his hand, one bill at a time.

Boiling corn for sale on the street

I walk on, slowly making my way through the crowd. At this point the street is too crowded for a bicycle or motorbike to drive. An array of smells float through the hot air; cooking food, stale water, cut watermelon, exhaust fumes that drift in from ahead and the ever-present dust are all mixed giving China its own distinctive odor.

She was always working

Every country has its own smell. I remember walking in Baltimore one day when suddenly I stopped. I was in Germany or so the odors said. I looked around and saw a German restaurant across the street. I remember Nancy sitting in a bus in Florida on the way to Disney Land telling me the people behind us were from Brazil. She had smelled the soap we always used when visiting her college roommate. This guess was confirmed when she began to eavesdrop and discovered they were speaking Portuguese.

Further along, on the sidewalk beside the major street I see cobblers and others repairing electrical and mechanical items. On my left, a woman I always see when I walk this way sits under her plastic awning repairing shoes. Shoes divided into two piles lay beside her; those she has repaired and those waiting for repairs. Head bowed she carefully nails a heel onto a black shoe. A young man and woman work beside her. They are here every time I pass regardless of the time of day or night. I wonder, do they ever sleep or eat?

On both sides of the street pool tables sit in the open, with no protection from the weather. Young men cigarettes dangling from their mouths play or watch. Shouts of encouragement, derision, or encouragement ring from observers and players alike. A young woman challenges a young man to play. The balls are racked, and she makes the break. A ball rolls into a pocket. Smiling confidently, she looks over the table, leans over and banks another ball into a side pocket. With an air of calm arrogance, she flashes her opponent a look of distain. I chuckled to myself. So, a female shark is hustling a male pool shark. I keep watching. She sinks three balls and I turn and walk toward the *Happy Lady's Restaurant.*

I walk carefully but still bump into people and I am bumped by others. Here bicyclists ride and I am brushed by a bicycle. I must step aside to avoid an oncoming bicycle. A red taxi slowly works its way along, its horn blaring. My right ear is numb from the horn. I let my finger run along the side window as it passes. I would like to twist the driver's neck for the constant horn blowing.

A little girl, about 8 or 9, walks toward me. She has a large smile on her face. Obviously, she is happy. She lifts her hand and I see her gnaw on a pig's foot. A man passes carrying two live chickens with their heads hanging down, their feet tied together. The chickens do not know they are to be supper for him and his family. A man on a bicycle passes with a watermelon in the basket attached to the handlebars. One hundred, two hundred, three hundred, a thousand people pass me as I walk. Children shout "Hollo". If I stop and speak to each one, I'll never arrive at the restaurant. An old woman approaches me, hands held together as if she is in prayer. She looks at me and moves her praying hands up and down as she asks for money. I look closely at her and realize she is not a beggar. Her clothes are new. There are no patches. She is a peasant woman come to the city and on seeing a foreigner hopes he was a soft touch and will give her a few coins or bills. She reaches out and touches my arm. I pass on. I look ahead and I see the smiling face of the happy lady. She sees me, throws up her arm and beckons me to come and eat. She jabbers to me in Chinese, and I jabber to her in English. I sat on a low stool under the red and blue plastic awning. I am sure she is asking me what I want to eat. I frown as if I am in deep thought. We both know what I am going to order. I smile as if I have just had a new idea, "Mien-Tao" I say, noodles and a Jin-Mei, a soft drink, to drink. Now two other expats and several Chinese friends join me. I am now set for the evening; good food, friendly talk, and time to watch Chinese street life swirl by.

The Happy Lady and Lori

One day Lori, a young American teaching English at NPU, told her that I called her the Happy Lady. A big smile crossed her face, and she gave me a thumbs up.

"Yes," she said, "I am a happy lady. I am going to rent a second place to expand my restaurant. Then I can have four woks. Now I have only one and sometimes people must wait too long for their food."

"Good luck," I said. "I think expanding is a good idea."

On my last full day at NPU I said goodbye to the Happy Lady. I hope she succeeded.

The Rose Garden Café

In 2000 when Nancy and I worked at NPU her restaurant was gone. I hope she moved to another location and had great success.

The Rose Garden Café Occasionally, we expats agree we wanted a hamburger, pizza, chicken tenders, salads, brownies, chocolate or carrot cake, and French fries. On those occasions we headed *to The Rose Garden Café*. We would catch a taxi as the café was located several miles from the campus. A Canadian woman, Carla, ran the café. Her Chinese husband was the cook, and she took care of the customers. They were good people having adopted three street children and using profits from the Rose Garden to help other street children go to school.

The Bitch

The Bitch ran an indoor restaurant between The Happy Lady and The Boss. She was always in a bad mood and showed it with shouts and rude remarks. The cook produced good food, but her personality left much to be desired. Thus, we expats tagged her restaurant as The Bitch. We did not go there often for the obvious reason that she was unpleasant to be around.

Kids Playing in the Dust

Normally Xi'an is quite dry, and the summer of 1995 was particularly dry and, thus, dusty. One day, as I was walking to the Happy Ladies for lunch, I stopped to watch toddlers playing while squatting on the dirt. They were having a great time playing and laughing, picking up dust and letting it trickle through their fingers, patting the dust, running their fingers through the dust, creating wiggly lines. I did not see any throwing it at others, nor did I see anyone making mudpies as there was no water available. Grandmothers sat or stood nearby gossiping as they watched the kids. My impression from this and other observations was that grandparents are the primary caretakers of children during the day. I do not remember ever seeing a young woman watching a toddler at play.

Crossing a busy street

Crossing a street in a Chinese city was always a challenge. Crossing a major street was a greater challenge. Bumper to bumper autos, trucks, buses come from both directions. Added to this mix were hundreds of bicycles. Well, this was true in 1995. With the increase of motorized vehicles in China such a crossing must be even more of a challenge.

There were no stoplights in many places where I needed to cross. Since most of those streets were heavily traveled four lane streets, I resorted to my often-used technique of standing eight to ten bodies down from traffic. When the folk up-traffic from me walked, I walked. When they stopped, I stopped. Often the stopping, standing, and waiting found us standing on a white line between lanes in the road. There we stood with traffic whizzing by on both sides of us until there was enough of a break in traffic that we could progress to the next waiting point. Usually, there was no possibility of crossing the street without stopping at least once before reaching the other side. There were times we had to stop three or four times before successfully reaching the far-away sidewalk. My thinking was that if I stood down-traffic and a car hit the pedestrians, those eight to ten people would serve as a buffer for me. I just might escape injury. I just might escape with no injury, unless, and I would have no idea of how, unless a flying body took me out as it descended to the street. I felt this was a minimum risk.

My wife, Nancy, who spent ten months in Xi'an in 2000-2001 developed another technique. She didn't depend on other people to keep her safe. She would stand, watch oncoming traffic and run to the white line in the center of a four-lane street when there were no cars. She would stand there with cars, trucks and bicycles whizzing past on each side of her until there was no traffic in the second lane. She would then run to the median strip and watch the next lane. After repeating this same slow plan across the final two lanes, she would be on her way. You know the old saying "Practice makes perfect". With this skill deep in her brain, she returned to Annapolis in late February. On her first trip to Graul's Grocery, she looked to her left, saw no cars and ran to the white line in the center of the four-lane Rowe Boulevard. There was a loud screeching of brakes and traffic in all four lanes came to a stop. It dawned on her that she had acted as if American drivers were used to someone standing on a white line when crossing a street. She never tried that again. She was now home and needed to revert to customs here.

Screams and a Machete

Sometimes people become angry. Sometimes when they are angry people become sullen, sometimes quiet, sometimes they walk away, sometimes they make threatening motions, sometimes they mumble, sometimes they talk and sometimes they scream. I am sure that both personality, temperament, and culture play a part in how a person acts when angry. Social status also plays a role in how anger is expressed. There are people who have self-control, who are successful in hiding their anger. Then there are those folks who do not have self-control and their anger is visible for all to see.

The voice is used in various ways to express anger. There is a calm, cold expression. There is a stern expression. There is a hard expression. There is a loud explosive reply. There is an all-out scream of outrage.

Anger in China

During my various times in China, many Chinese friends told me that, "We like quiet people." I have found this an interesting comment as, to me, the Chinese are, for the most part, not quiet. Yes, there are quiet individuals, but the culture is neither a quiet one nor is the language. Because of the tones in the language, the sound of Chinese being spoken by two or more people sounds as if they are arguing to ears used to English. It was a hot day in August. Four of us expats and several Chinese friends were on our way to The Boss restaurant for lunch. Leaving the campus, we turned right, walking past The Happy Lady's restaurant and then right to follow the street, perhaps a hundred yards, where we crossed the intersection of a busy four-lane street. Along the way we passed peasants who had peddled their small tricycles into the city, carrying vegetables, fruit, and other farm produce.

Screaming

Now I have heard and seen Chinese screaming at each other on several occasions. Usually, this comes about following bicycle accidents.

Nancy and I, while hiking in the Fragrant Hills Park in the northwestern part of Beijing in 1989 saw two men screaming at each other; they almost came to blows before a policeman stepped in to calm them. He led the men into a small building. Nancy, whose Chinese is much better than mine, told me the policeman said several times, "Stop! What will the foreigners think?"

We expats and Chinese friends had just successfully crossed the street. Suddenly behind us, we heard screaming, angry screaming, angry at the top of their lungs, between two men. Others on the street turned to see what was happening.

As I watched one man snatched a machete from the other and grabbed him by his hair and pulled his head down and forward as he raised the machete. The screaming continued. I could not understand what was being screamed. There was no doubt that both people had totally lost their tempers and were screaming, in no uncertain terms, clean or obscene. My guess is the words were often obscene. I felt both individuals were going to suffer from a sore throat and laryngitis.

"Dear God," Ruth whispered.

"Oh, no," Lori exclaimed.

"Oh, man," I thought, "am I about to see a man's head chopped off?" I feared that was about to happen.

Two women stood nearby. I assumed they were the wives of the two men. One stood watching with a stern look on her face. The other stepped forward, holding her hands out in a pleading way. I could not hear what she was saying. Was she pleading for the man with the knife to stop or was she encouraging him to kill the thief?

The man lowered the machete, kept screaming, raised the machete, lowered it, raised it, lowered it.

The thought of stepping between the men never entered my mind and no one on their side made a move toward them. All talking, all activity had ceased. Only the screaming continued.

At times like this, the human brain filters out the extraneous and concentrates on the immediate and time seems to stand still.

My brain cut off the sound of traffic passing. My attention, everyone's attention was centered on the two men. We were all frozen in place, watching with bated breath. What was the man going to do?

Raising the machete and lowering it continued for at least a minute or two. All this time he continued screaming. The women continued, one standing and watching the other pleading. We expats and friends watched, holding our breath, fearful of what we might see and seemingly cemented into the sidewalk, not moving nor speaking.

Finally, the man lowered the machete pushed the other away, spun on his heel and walked to his tricycle truck.

"That was terrifying," one in our group said. "I was scared to death."

I felt the same. Phil, an American teaching English at the university spoke, "Well now that the fun is over, can we go eat?"

"Yes," all of us responded.

Changing money in Xi'an

When a person goes into a bank, a post office, a government building, or even a store in China, they cannot know what they will find. Laws, if there are any, have no influence unless they serve the person waiting on the client.

One day Cindy, a young American woman, who was teaching English asked Ruth and me to accompany her to the central bank as she needed to cash several traveler's checks. She needed Ruth to interpret for her. I can't remember why she wanted me to accompany her. But I did.

We rode a city bus and got off at the Bell Tower. Then we walked to the central bank on East Street. I had cashed traveler's checks there several times and had experienced no problems. For Cindy today was different.

We entered the bank and walked to the window marked "Foreign Exchange." A young man sat on the other side of the barred window. As Cindy approached, he motioned in an unfriendly wave of his hand that she should turn around and make the exchange at the window behind us. We turned and saw a young woman sitting there watching us.

Ruth said to Cindy, "Give her your passport and the checks you need to have cashed."

Cindy did as Rush advised. The bank teller spoke in rapid Chinese. "What did she say?" Cindy asked.

Ruth turned to Cindy. "She said she is not the right person to cash the checks. The woman to her left is who you need to deal with."

There were several Chinese customers at that window. We waited. Finally, we got to the head of the line. The bank teller sat looking at us but said nothing. There was no "May I help you?" She silently stared at us.

We stood there five to ten seconds before Ruth said, "Cindy, slide the checks under the bar and your passport as well."

Cindy did as Ruth said. The woman took the checks and checked the signatures. Turning she handed them to another woman who counted out the money. This lady handed them to a third woman who counted the money again and laid it on a desk behind the first woman who continued to sit, staring at us.

Ruth, speaking with an authoritative voice told her, "The money is ready. Give it to us." The woman turned, picked up the money, counted it, and slid it to Cindy. This simple task took twenty minutes. All this time the first young man we had approached sat talking to a young woman totally ignoring us.

Day Trip to the Xiang Jiao Temple

At 8:00 a.m. on June 25, 1995, I met Wu Xiang, one of his friends, and Janet, his friend's daughter. I had met Janet a few days before and at that time she said her favorite book in English was *Little Women*. Currently, she was reading the writings of Mark Twain. Janet was a bright 12-year-old who spoke flawless English. As soon as I met her, I was sure she had lived in the States. I was right! Janet's father had spent 3 years at the University of Utah where Janet lived for 14 months. She said her English was zero when she arrived in the US. She now spoke with almost no accent.

Janet, her father, and Wu Xiang

A university car picked us up and drove us to the Xiang Jiao Temple. For all of us it was our first time visiting this temple. The complex, also known as the Monastery of Flourishing Teaching, is 12.5 miles south of Xi'an near the 8,500-foot tall Zhong Nan Mountains. The flat countryside gave way to progressively larger hills. We passed several peasant villages as well as harvested wheat fields. Other fields of rape were green and would be harvested in late summer. The car turned off the blacktop road onto a well-graded dirt road that led to the temple complex. The driver let us out of the car at the main gate. Stepping through the gate. I turned around. Looking outward from the main gate I was pleased with the beautiful view down across a valley to the high mountains in the South called the Zhong Nan. The mountains beckoned me, but I had no way of visiting them. It was possible the government had declared them off-limits to foreigners, something I had experienced before.

The Reclining Buddha

The temple was divided into three courtyards, Front Courtyard, East Courtyard and West Courtyard. Structures stand densely in the Front Courtyard; they are Mountain Gate, Bell and Drum Towers, Devajara Hall (Daxiong-baodian) and Preach Hall. Daxiong-baodian is very grand, where a bronze Sakyamuni statue sits in the middle, in front of which is a 2 meters high white jade joss presented by Burma. The East Courtyard is the Storehouse of Buddhism scriptures. The West Courtyard is the Stupa Courtyard. There are dagoba that contained the bones of Xuanzang and two small dagobas contained the bones of Xuanzang's two disciples. Xuanang is the 7th century Buddhist monk who brought Buddhist scripture to China.

The grave of the monk, Xuan Zang, who brought the Buddhist scriptures from India to China, is here. He divided his time, living here and at the Famen Temple 75 miles west of Xi'an. The famous story, *Journey to the West*, was inspired by his journey to and from India. Xiang Jiao was one of the nicest temples I visited. Construction of the temple began in 669 A.D. during the Tang Dynasty, 618 - 684 and 705 - 984. It is off the beaten track and the only foreign tourists who come here are from Japan. Japanese Buddhists had erected a stone stele with an inscription telling of the eternal friendship between the

Japanese and the Chinese. It was a large complex and well-kept with lush green grounds and maintained buildings. At Xiang Jiao I saw my first recumbent Buddha. I wondered if there was a meaning associated with him reclining. Later I discovered the recumbent Buddha signifies the death of the Buddha. Covered in gold leaf the Buddha was at least twenty feet long. I knew that the swastika was an ancient

The Many Armed Buddha

symbol. Still, I was caught off-guard seeing one on the Buddha's chest. In Hinduism, the swastika is a clockwise symbol. From Sanskrit the work carries the meaning of well-being. The Nazi swastika is a counterclockwise symbol and has become a symbol of bigotry and hatred.

The temple is set on a steep hill near the mountains. The viewing area was small. This prevented me from taking a picture of the entire statue. I stepped back as far as I could and snapped a photo. Incense sticks smoldered in front of the Buddha.

There was also the many armed Buddha, Avalokiteśvara the teacher of compassion.

Hundreds of sweet-smelling roses, some taller than my head, were in bloom in the gardens and lined brick pathways. Artistically placed bamboo of various kinds grew on the grounds. The bamboo and trees supplied welcome shade from the summer sun. In full sun the day was uncomfortably warm. Except for several monks, we were alone, free to wander to our hearts delight.

Lunch could be bought but we did not stay long enough to eat there. I would have liked to eat there as I had enjoyed the meal with Wang at the monastery near Suzhou.

Peasant Village

Leaving the monastery, we walked down the hill toward a peasant village. Harvested wheat lay on the flat roofs. Men and women were working, raking the wheat, turning it to dry evenly in the sun. Wheat and other grains were also drying on the ground and on village streets. Peasants raked the grains of wheat, turning them to evenly dry in the sun.

Raking grains of wheat to dry

We stopped and my two hosts talked with a peasant. He told us the wheat harvest that year was good, but because of the severe lack of rain, the corn harvest was going to be terrible.

Talking with the peasant farmer

Almost no rain had fallen in May or June. Several weeks later I heard that fights had broken out between villages over water. As one person said to me, "When there is no water, people quickly become desperate and violent."

Turning off the road we walked through several of the dusty streets of the village. Several new brick homes showed that recent times had been good. We met a man and his wife walking toward us. The wife was carrying her 15-month-old grandson. Wheat had been spread on the dusty street to dry before being stored. We stopped and my two friends spoke to him. He invited us into his home. A new brick home stood inside his walled courtyard. To the right of the front door was a well.

Wu asked, "How deep is the well?"

The peasant scratched his chin before speaking, "About thirty meters. I dug it myself."

I was impressed, thirty meters is 98.5 feet. No wooden ladder is that long, and I wondered if he used a rope ladder or just a rope with evenly spaced knots on which to climb and descent.

He invited us into the house. Stepping through the front door we found ourselves in a centered room. There was a single room through a door on both the right and left side of the room in which we were standing. Bags of wheat leaned against one wall in the center room. Several bicycles and two-wheeled carts were stored in the room. I was not surprised when he said they stored them in the house to prevent someone from stealing them. He and his wife used the room on the right. The floors were made of packed mud and straw bricks. The bricks appeared laid with no binding agent.

Their room had a bed on the right with a bamboo pad lying over it. Bamboo is cooler during the heat of summer than cloth. A cabinet stood at the foot of the bed against a wall. His daughter-in-law walked into the room and placed food in the cabinet. To me, it looked like coarse cornbread. A small table stood near the bed, and this is where they squat to eat. I saw only one chair. Men in Shaanxi often carry their food outside, squat on the bare earth and eat. A black and white TV sat on a table at the far end of the room. It sat in the bottom part of the Styrofoam container it had come packaged in when they bought it. Beautiful calendar pictures hung nailed to the walls. A large free-standing closet stood near the TV. We declined his offer of cigarettes as none of us smoked.

The room to the left of the center room is for his son and their daughter-in-law. This room held their bed as well as a free-standing closet. Calendar pictures hung from nails on the walls. There was no TV in this room. I saw no refrigerator, no fan, and no other electrical appliances.

The house has two upstairs rooms. They rented these rooms to two doctors. My guess is these were two 'barefoot doctors'. Barefoot doctors are men and women from peasant villages with a minimal medical education. Many never completed high school. Their medical studies lasted from six months to a year. Disease prevention and curing simple complaints was the primary goal of the program. The program was coming to an end by 1995, as everything in China was moving toward a free market system. The reduction of government funds for medical services resulted in peasants having to pay for services and this was a hardship.

The man shrugged and said, "Doctors are not very important to anyone in the village."

I was not sure what he meant by this; did he mean they were not good doctors or that few went to see them regardless of their medical need? Perhaps as they do not help harvest crops or work in gardens, they have little social standing. Perhaps their pay is so low they are not desirable mates for the young people of the village.

The Mama pig

Finally, we walked outside. A few chickens were running around. A deep hole, ten or so feet deep and ten by ten feet square was the home of a large pig with several piglets.

I carefully avoided walking near the sunken pigpen, as I was sure anyone who fell into this pit might not live to get out. The pig was large, black, and wrinkled. Mother pigs can be vicious when angered or when protecting their young. This mother did not appear friendly.

Visiting this peasant home reminded me of poor people I had known in Southern West Virginia when I was a kid. However, this newly constructed home was nicer than the houses of the poor in Appalachia. Many of those homes were in ill repair with rickety front-porches and steps. I wondered how or if this peasant family heated their home in the winter. There was no air conditioning. To me there was no question that life here was not easy.

Leaving the village, we climbed into the car and returned to the university.

Chinese woman with a problem

It was a beastly hot day in August. Except for lunch, I worked all day editing conference papers. Walking out of the guesthouse I thought I would walk to the Happy Ladies for supper. I stepped out of the door and a blast of heat met me. I stopped, first looking at the guesthouse gate and then at the guesthouse restaurant. "I'm tired," I thought, "and it is hot, and I do not want to walk through the heat. I'll go to the guesthouse restaurant. It is just a few steps away.

I walked into the restaurant. One of the waitresses pointed to a table. There was no freedom of choice in seating here. I sat, between two young Chinese men and a young Chinese woman. Food served family style was brought to the table. As always there was a bowl of white rice that we were to share. The men served themselves and handed the rice to me. I took some rice and handed it to the young woman. As she took it she said, "Thank you." There was also a pork dish and several vegetable dishes for us to share. We began eating.

In a minute or so she asked me a question. Her English was excellent with almost no accent. We began talking. It was one of those rare situations where, almost at once, it seemed we had known each other for years. She was visiting NPU for several days and was to meet a friend there. The men finished their meal, got up, and left. Now, she and I were the only customers in the restaurant. We continued talking. The minutes rolled past. "Maybe we should leave," I said. "The staff probably would like to close and go home. She agreed. "I would like to talk more," I said. "Would you like to go to the corner store and have some ice cream?" I asked.

"Yes, I would," she replied.

We expats called the store the corner store because it stood on a corner on the campus. There were outside tables with chairs where we could sit and eat. As we sat and ate the ice cream we continued talking. I do not remember the exact conversation but somehow religion was mentioned. I said, "I am a Christian."

She sat up straight with a surprised look. "You are a Christian!"

"Yes I am."

"I need to talk with you," she said. "I have a big problem." I studied in Germany last year. While I was there, I started attending a Bible study and became a Christian. We had a long discussion about God and being a Christian. I became convinced that she was a Christian. "This is a big problem for me, because of where I work and because of my parents."

"Tell me more," I said.

"Because of what happened to them my mother and father are terrified about almost everything. They are Party members. If I tell them I am a Christian, they will denounce me and turn me into the authorities and only a Party member can have my job. I could never travel outside China again. What am I to do? If I lose my job, I will not be able to be employed again and the authorities will punish me. Becoming a Christian would be considered a serious political mistake. I don't know what to do."

"Let me think," I said.

We sat quietly for several minutes. Finally, I said, "Here is my advice. Pray to God telling Him your problem, though He already knows. Ask for guidance. My other thought is that you may be exactly where God wants you to be. You are in a position where you can influence others. If you were not there, you could not influence them. Go home, go to work, and wait for an answer."

"That is good advice," she said. "I believe that God brought us together. "When I bought my train ticket home, I did not notice they scheduled me a day later than I wanted to travel. I thought about returning and exchanging it for the day I had planned on traveling. Then I decided to keep the ticket and stay here at NPU until I leave. Also, I never speak to strangers, especially foreigners. But today, in the restaurant I surprised myself and asked you a question.

She returned to her home and continued her work. Within a short period of time, an opportunity came her way to work for an international organization that required her to travel outside of China. She is safe in being a Christian in her current work.

Last Month in Xi'an

Cool Weather

October arrived with warm weather holding firm. One day I had shorts on as I left the guesthouse to go to lunch. As usual I was going with several expats and Chinese friends. One Chinese friend, Zhou Li Ping, looked surprised when she saw me in shorts.

"Are you crazy?" she asked.

"Maybe," I replied. "Why do you ask?"

Staring at me she exclaimed, "It is October. Everyone puts on long underwear and long pants. Don't you know that?"

"No, I do not know that. It is hot enough that shorts are comfortable. Long pants? Maybe I could wear them but certainly not long underwear."

"Well," she said, "I hope you do not get sick."

As October moved along, the weather became cool, and I broke out my long pants and long sleeve shirts. Rain also arrived, sometimes a mist and sometimes a downpour. The time of shorts was past, gone for the year.

I had no responsibilities during the conference and do not remember anything about the papers presented or the people who were presenters. Once the conference was over all my time was free time. Now I had time to travel. The Waiban helped me purchase train tickets and a ticket to travel by boat up the Yangtze River, through the Three Gorges to Chongqing and then to Guizhou to visit Sun Hai's parents. I was excited.

Yangtze River Trip

Wuhan
A is for Apple

I stood at the entrance of the Wuhan train station, a surprisingly small entrance considering that Wuhan is one of the largest cities in the world and the capital of Hubei Provence. I had traveled to Wuhan by train from Xi'an, a trip of almost twenty-four hours. I chose to stand at the wall just outside the entrance. I was sure it would be easy to see me, a foreigner, a big-nose foreign devil, standing there.

The sister of one of my friends, Yu Hailing, in Xi'an was to meet me and guide me to Wuhan University. I was to spend a night there before boarding a ship for a cruise up the Yangtze River. I had never met the young woman who was to meet me, but I figured that there would not be that many foreigners standing at the entrance. I was right. I was the only such person. A sea of people passed me in both directions. Thousands of people use a station such as this every day. Most paid no attention to me.

I stood there for about five minutes, a little concerned, but not worried, that I would not be found. Suddenly an elderly beggar woman appeared in front of me. Her hands were clasped together as if in prayer moving them up and down. This is the motion beggars use when asking for money. She had a deeply lined face, a limp in her step and was dressed in a ragged black dress.

In addition to my backpack, I had a brown paper bag of goodies including several beautiful apples. "Ah," I thought, "just the thing." Reaching into the bag I selected one of the apples and handed it to her. She took the apple and held it up before her face. Slowly a beautiful smile appeared. Quickly the apple disappeared into the bag she carried. Quickly she bowed to me and disappeared into

Just as she disappeared a well-dressed middle-aged man walked past me. Catching my eye, he gave me a happy smile and a thumbs-up.

Several minutes later Yu Hailing's sister and a friend arrived to take me to the university they attended. I was staying at the university guest house. When we arrived, I checked into the guest house. The Foreign Affairs Office had reserved me a room. Also, they had given one of their young employees the task of taking me to the river front and making sure I got on the Yangtze Princess that would take me up the river to Chongqing.

I remember nothing about the guest house or what I did until it was time for me to meet Sun to go to the river.

Waiting for the Waiban man

Surrounded by lush semi-tropical plants, I stood in the shade of the university guard house. A warm breeze brushed my face as I waited for Sun, the young man from the Waiban to arrive. Though it was Sunday, normally a day of rest for everyone at the university, Sun had been given the task of going with me to the Yangtze River boat that was to take me through the Three Gorges and on to Chongqing.

"I wonder why he was given the job," I thought, "I bet it is because he's single and the newest member of the staff. So, he is the easy answer for weekend work." I chuckled to myself at the thought, the new person the world over draws the extra work. "Well," I thought, "I hope he doesn't mind seeing the 'old foreigner' to the ship. I'll give him a good tip. That should supply solace if any is needed."

Soon, above an iron fence, I saw Sun's head bobbing as he walked toward me. Seeing me as he rounded the corner, his hand flew up; a big smile crossed his face. "Hello Bill," he called. "I see you are ready."

"Yes," I called back. "I always like to be ready. I don't like to have to rush. I'm glad to see you. I'd be lost without your help."

I put my backpack on and walked to meet him. "Where do we catch a taxi?"

"Here, at the corner. One will come along soon," he replied. "I never have to wait long."

Sun was right. In just a few minutes a taxi appeared driving down the long entrance way to the university. A man and a woman sat in the back seat.

"Don't worry," he said, "the taxi will be back in a few minutes. When that couple gets out, he will come back. He saw us and knew we need a ride."

Again, Sun was right. In a few minutes the taxi returned. Sun waved his hand. The taxi stopped and the driver waved at us. "Get in the front," Sun said, "I'll sit in the back."

"No," I replied, "you sit in front. You may need to tell the driver where to turn. It will be easier if you are in front."

Sun thought for a moment, "OK," he said. Opening the door, he climbed into the taxi.

I tossed my backpack onto the seat and climbed in. With a last look over my shoulder I said a mental "Goodbye" to the university.

At the end of the road leading to the university gate the taxi turned right. Soon we were surrounded by six lanes of Wuhan city traffic. We passed the Wuhan railway station and then crossed the Yangtze River bridge. I noticed the day before from the train window guards with automatic rifles at both ends of the bridge. Again, I saw the armed guards. So, at least four guards are posted here all the time. Two on the railroad level and two on the vehicular level.

"Hmmm," I wondered, "why are they guarding the bridge? I asked Sun.

"They are here to protect the bridge," Sun replied.

"What are they protecting it from," I ask.

"I don't know," he replied. "Bad people I guess."

I scratched my head and thought, "What terrorists would be fool enough to travel this far from the sea to blow up a bridge? Aren't there targets just as tempting in Shanghai or Beijing? Is there that much dissatisfaction in this part of China, or is it a way of keeping a few soldiers occupied?"

Once across the bridge the taxi left the wide street, turning onto a narrow street running parallel to the Yangtze River. River barges piled the river.

All this time, for about forty-five minutes Sun and the taxi driver had kept up a rapid-fire conversation. Occasionally Sun would turn in his seat and ask me a question and then return to Wuhan dialect while talking to the driver. I know a little Mandarin, but there was nothing in the Wuhan dialect which meant anything to me. However, it seemed obvious I was the center of the conversation. After all, with a foreigner in the cab, what else is there to talk about?

Y is for Yangtze Princess

It was almost 6:00 p.m. and the sun was sinking low when Sun and I climbed out of the taxi. With trail mix in a zip lock bag and two bottles of mineral water in my journalist jacket I was again well prepared for another adventure in China. I noticed a tall clock tower rising above an office building. Other than at train stations, clock towers were rare in China. Sun and I walked down a short street toward the water to a pier that extended out 100 feet into the flowing muddy water of the river. The Yangtze is not as silt laden as the Yellow River, but annually it carries thousands of tons of silt. Much of this rich silt is deposited becoming the riverbank as high water recedes from the wet summer season. I saw deposits twelve or more feet high as the ship traveled upstream. These silt deposits are used as vegetable gardens. The Yangtze Princess, scheduled to leave at 9:00 p.m., was not there. Boarding was to begin at 7:00 p.m. I knew we had not missed the boat as the clock was just striking 6:00. There was nothing to do but settle down and wait. Other than a few workers Sun and I were alone on the dock.

"Hmm," I said, "I wonder where the boat is?"

"I don't know," Sun said, "there are some workmen. I'll see if they know anything."

Quickly Sun walked toward the workmen. After a brief conversation, he returned to where I was standing. "They say that the ship is late in arriving because of fog."

"Fog," I thought, "I wonder where they ran into fog. I could see for miles. There was no fog." I smiled to myself feeling sure that fog was not the reason. It was a good excuse and much more face-saving than simply saying, "The Yangtze Princess is behind schedule."

I leaned my backpack against a metal fence. "Well," I said, "there's not much to do but wait. Sun, you go on back to the university. This is the right pier. There is no point in you wasting your time standing here with me. Certainly, you have more interesting things to do on a Sunday evening. I'll be fine."

"No," Sun said with a shrug, "I will stay with you. It is my job."

"I appreciate you staying with me, but really, I'll be fine. I don't mind if you go back. It's Sunday evening, time for you to have fun."

Sun shook his head, "No, I must stay. I must see that you get on the boat."

I could see it was pointless to continue urging Sun to return to the university. I'm sure that if he left and for some reason I did not get on the ship, he would be in trouble. Also, I figured that he really didn't know why the ship was late and had no idea when it would arrive. That led me to think the worst case could be that we would both have to return to the university for the night and that I could not board until the morning ... or later.

Ladies from England

Gradually the evening twilight faded, and we were left in darkness. I noticed a taxi pull up. Two women, one young the one elderly got out. The driver sat their suitcases on the pier, took his money and drove away.

The younger woman approached and with a decided English accent said, "Excuse me, is this the pier at which we are to catch the Yangtze Princess?"

Nodding his head Sun said, "Yes, it is. Unfortunately, it is late arriving. I hope it will be here shortly."

"I am glad to know we are in the right place. Is there a place where my grandmother may sit? She is quite tired. It has been a long day."

"I'm afraid not," Sun replied.

"Oh dear, well, we will just have to wait I suppose." She then turned and walked to her grandmother.

My stomach was telling me it was well past time for supper. I had thought I would board on schedule and either eat a meal on the ship or eat from my store of food in my backpack. I opened my backpack and pulled out my five pounds of trail mix. Opening the Zip-lock bag I offered some to Sun.

"What is it?" he said suspiciously. I understood his suspicion very well as I had, on several occasions, been offered and eaten unknown foods.

"We call it trail mix," I said. "It's a mixture of nuts and dried fruit. I always carry it with me when I'm traveling."

With an "I guess I have to do this to be polite" shrug Sun took a handful. There was enough light reflecting from the nearby street for me to see a surprised look come over his face. "This is good," he exclaimed. I was surprised that Sun had not refused at least two times. Refusing twice and accepting on the third offer is standard in the Chinese culture.

"I think so," I replied. "The two ladies are probably hungry. Let's join them."

I offered them some trail mix. At first, they politely refused, but finally took some for a snack.

"Thank you," the grandmother said. "I was becoming somewhat hungry."

Crowd Gathers

The four of us talked, stared at the flowing river, and talked more. Not being a night person, I was getting tired by this time and hoped that I would not have to wait much longer. All of us were tired and though no one said so we were all hoping the Yangtze Princess would soon come into view.

About an hour later a large tourist bus pulled into the dock area. "I hope that's a good sign," I said. "Maybe they have more information about the boat than we do."

Sun wiped his face. "Yes," he replied, "I imagine the tour company has been in touch with the ship. I think it will be here soon now."

Sun was right. About ten minutes later a large riverboat came into view. Slowly the ship approached the pier. Ropes were thrown from the ship and wrapped around large posts securing the ship. Workers quickly ran out a gangplank onto the pier.

"You will have to wait until the people leave the boat," Sun said. "They will let you know when you can get onboard."

"Well," I said turning to Sun, "the boat is here. There really is no need for you to stay longer. Go on to your home. It's late."

"All right," he replied.

"Here is a little bit for all your trouble and help," I said handing him twenty RMB, about $2.50. He could buy a good meal with that amount.

"You don't have to give me anything," he protested.

"I know," I said, "but you have been helpful. Buy yourself a good meal. You must be very hungry by now."

Taking the money Sun thanked me. We shook hands and he left, going back to the university having done his duty of seeing the foreigner safely to the ship.

Soon all the onboard passengers were off the ship. We waited while the ship's crew readied for the upstream journey to Chongqing.

As each person boarded their name was checked and given a slip of paper with their cabin number. I boarded at 9:00 p.m., walked across the deck entering a hallway making my way to cabin #406. It was a small room with two twin beds, two closets and a small toilet and shower. All cabins had large, curtained windows. Happily, I had no roommate. This surprised me as on trains there are always four people in every soft-sleeper compartment. Foreigners were encouraged to always travel soft sleeper on Chinese trains.

The university foreign affairs office in Wuhan bought my ticket paying the foreign teacher's price. My cost was $430.00 instead of the regular price of $590.00. A nice saving of money. By the time I settled, it was 10:00 p.m. The Yangtze Princess was still at the dock. I saw no sign we would leave anytime soon. It had been a long day, and I went to bed sleeping soundly until about 5:30 a.m. The next morning.

I had never seen so many waterfalls in any place I had visited as along the Yangtze River. It seems there was always one, and often more, waterfalls in sight at any one point in time. Fairly often three or more waterfalls were visible. Some water tumbled long distances before breaking on the rocks below. Other falls were lacy falls tumbling over rocks as the water descended into the river below. We passed one town which was filled with waterfalls. The bluffs rose high above the river, but obviously there is a lot of water coming down from the invisible mountains beyond.

Vegetables growing beside the Yangtze

Vegetables Growing

Wherever the land is flat enough along the Yangtze River peasants plant vegetables on the mud deposited by the last flood. On steep hillsides I saw all types of vegetables growing, the green of the vegetable leaf contrasting with the brown of the deposited silt. This told me that, though this region receives lots of rain, it is not a hard-driving rain that would cause severe erosion. I imagine that in cool weather vegetables, like cabbage, are grown, even in the winter. It seems to me the probability of seeing the rewards of a person's labor is much greater with the vegetables than with fishing in the river. As we moved upstream toward Chongqing, I saw men standing on the rocks of the shore fishing with nets attached to bamboo poles. It seemed a futile effort as I never saw a man catch a fish.

On the Yangtze

Path cut from the stone cliff

I slept soundly and woke a little after 05:00. It was dawn. The growing light from the sun woke me. I got up, shaved, and showered. Now I was ready for the day. At 06:00 I walked out on the deck. The air was misty and chilly. Only one other passenger was up and out at that time. We acknowledged each other with a nod. He turned and stared upriver. I looked all around.

There were low mountains in the distance and little else of interest. However, the Yangtze is a busy river. Two tour ships were following us, and other river craft were going both up and down-stream. The Yangtze has been an artery of commerce for centuries. In ancient times coolies pulled the riverboats upstream. A large rope was tied to the prow of the ship. Toward the end of the rope small ropes were spliced to the large one. Each was spliced to itself forming a loop. This loop went over the coolie's shoulder. Thus, large numbers of coolies strained moving the riverboat slowly upstream. In mountainous areas paths had been chiseled into the cliff sides. In many places the cliffs are so sheer that the trail was like a half circle. Not only was the work of pulling the ships murderously hard there was the ever-present danger of slipping or being pulled off the path and falling to the rocks below. My guess is that many men lost their life from falls and early deaths from overwork.

Wakeup Call

I returned to my cabin. Beautiful music from the Chinese concerto, *Butterfly Lovers*[xvi], came over the speakers in my room at 07:00. This was and is my favorite Chinese music. Indeed, it is the favorite of many Chinese also. Soon I heard people in the hallway.

Breakfast

Everyone was friendly and looking forward to going through the three gorges as we gathered to eat.

Breakfast was a mixture of Chinese and Western food and the first real breakfast food I had eaten in several months. I had been eating peanut butter and jelly sandwiches while at NPU, in Xi'an. Tea was served as the morning drink. Unlike a trip in 1986 there was no beer. On that trip four liters of beer waited on the table at each meal, including breakfast as well as four bottles of a soft orange drink that we tagged "orange death".

Dining room

There was one sitting for each meal. All passengers were together with one table set up for foreigners. In Mandarin, it is impossible for Chinese to be called a foreigner. There are 'inside people', inside the wall and 'outside people', everyone else. There were a few of us outside people onboard; a man from Holland, the young woman and her grandmother from England and a couple from the US and two others. The man from Holland worked for an American company and was accompanied by his Chinese wife. He was her boss until she moved and took a job with Motorola. I did not ask if his company had a rule against spouses working together.

The day's schedule was:

    ◇ 7:00-8:00 a.m. breakfast
    ◇ 10:00 a.m. explanation of the schedule for today
    ◇ 12:00-3:30 p.m. ashore at the Yueyang Tower
    ◇ 6:30 p.m. Captain's cocktail party and welcoming speech
    ◇ 7:00 p.m. evening meal.

Swimming pool

I could not fathom why, but the small ship's swimming pool was partially filled with river water today. As the silt began to settle to the bottom the pool was pumped dry. This left a layer of silt on the pool floor. To me it was an excellent illustration of what will happen when the Three Georges Dam is completed, and water begins to form a lake several hundred miles in length. The lake behind the dam will fill with silt.

Mahjong

Always three or four tables were filled with Chinese playing mahjong. I noticed one group spent the entire day sitting playing this popular game. Perhaps this was one of the high-stakes games. A Chinese lady, whose husband is an American, told me there are several high-stakes games being played. I did not know how much money was needed for a game to be considered high stakes. I certainly was not going to sit down at a table to find out. There were a few card games as well, but not as many as mahjong.

Captain's Party

Before our evening meal there was the captain's party. He gave a short welcoming speech. In closing, he pointed to two tables of drinks and a long buffet table filled with a variety of Chinese food. I was amazed watching the Chinese travelers rush to the food table. It was a feeding frenzy. Few Chinese picked up drinks. Instead, they crowded the buffet, eating fast and picking up more. Conversations did not exist. We almond-eyed westerners sat together, ate a bit of food we somehow had gotten, and had a few drinks. Fortunately for me there were some non-alcoholic drinks. The feeding frenzy amazed me as our evening meal was to be served in the dining room in 30 minutes. The day ended, and I returned to my room for a night of rest.

Channel Markers and Dikes

Channel marker

The Yangtze channel markers look like small row boats with a three-foot tower at midship. A light is at the apex of the tower. The markers are anchored to the river bottom with a lead that allows the boat to rise and fall as the water level changes.

Because of the dikes there were stretches along the river where the land was hidden from view. It gave me a feeling of being on the Mississippi River, but then I would see a water buffalo, a person with a bamboo carrying pole, or a small sampan and know that this was China. One quarter of all the people in China live in the Yangtze drainage area. This was more people than in the entire United States.

We were still in flat country with paddies stretching to the horizon. Dikes ran along both sides of the river. The river facing side was at times lined with stones, at other times by soil. Occasionally I saw sections of the dike that had been damaged by high water during the summer. It did not appear that water had flowed over the top of the dike flooding the fields beyond. The flat countryside would give way to hills and mountains later this day as we approached the town of Yichang and the site of the then under construction Three Gorges Dam. The Xiling gorge begins just beyond Yichang.

Small ferries cross the Yangtze, each capable of carrying one or two trucks. I saw one such ferry, capable of carrying 2 trucks, approaching the docking area. On shore waiting were 12 trucks. Those at the end will have to wait for the 6th trip. Yesterday I saw a line of trucks extending from the river up a hill and out of sight beyond. I wondered if trucks at the back of this line would have to wait until the next day before their turn to cross the river would come.

Yueyang Tower

After lunch, we docked and visited the Yueyang Tower. Dating from the Three Kingdoms period (220–280) the Yueyang Tower overlooks Dongting Lake where a famous battle, the Battle of the Red Cliffs, took place in 208.

The tower, which to my western eye looked like a pagoda, overlooks Lake Dongting. Legend has it that during the Three Kingdoms Period, one of the military leaders stood in the tower and watched and directed his naval forces as they trained.

Feudo – the Ghost City, Gateway to Hell

The Yangtze Princess stopped at a dock in Feudo, the Ghost City. We were told the gateway to hell is located here. This led to many buildings, temples, and other structures dedicated to the underworld, or hell being constructed. An open cable car took several of us to the top of a small mountain where the tower stood. By chance, I was seated with our local guide, Sarah. As we rode, we talked.

I asked her, "Were you born in the Ghost City?"

"No," Sarah replied. "I was born in a small town. It is about three hours away by boat. About twenty miles."

"Where did you study?" Her English was very good.

"I went to the Chengdu Normal University. After I graduated, I joined the CITS (China International Travel Service) and was sent here. That was two and a half years ago. We have a staff of forty people. Lots of tourist ships stop here, and we have interpreters in English, French, Japanese, German, and several other languages. In a few days, a ship will arrive and will have over three hundred American tourists onboard."

"Do you like working here?"

She thought a few seconds before answering. "I like the work, but not the town."

I found that an interesting answer. "Why?" I asked.

Frowning she said, "Because the people here are not friendly to anyone not born here."

"That is a shame," I said. "Can you move to another city?"

Nodding her head she replied, "Yes, I could. But to move I would have to pay my work unit ¥10,000 RMB. With my salary that is impossible.

We had arrived at the top of the mountain. Sarah gathered the group together and led us to see the historical sites.

Loading coal

We passed a small town. I saw a line of people unloading coal from a barge. Each person had a bamboo pole across one shoulder. Suspended from each end of the pole was bamboo split woven, shovel shaped container. Each container was about a foot and a half wide and two to two and a half feet long. I will call them a basket. When a person's baskets were filled that person turned and trudged down a narrow plank to the shore. After a short walk he dumped his load onto a growing pile. I also saw a barge being loaded, in the same manner, with red earth. It must take hours and hours to unload or load a barge in this way. Backbreaking work had not ended by 1995.

Along the shore some areas were lined with trees. Flat fields, being worked by peasants with water buffalo stretched out in other areas. Occasionally the buffalo were led to the river, letting them walk into the cooling water and drink silt laden water. Only men and water buffalo were working in the fields. Unlike other places in China, I had passed through; no women were working the land. As I travelled out of Hefei to Suzhou, I saw rice paddies with only women working in them. Wang, my traveling companion at that time said it was a big problem in many parts of China as all the men had left, going to big cities searching for cash paying jobs. The only tractors I saw were small ones being used to load a barge.

After the ship docked that evening, I saw local fishermen selling fish to the chief cook of the Yangtze Princess. We had been served small fish for breakfast. Obviously, we were going to be served fish for our evening meal. We were not limited to just fish. Other dishes and vegetables were served resulting in a good selection of foods to choose from. Our local guide for this area, a young woman from Xi'an, told me that the most famous dishes in this region are fish. I saw many fish drying on the roofs of small boats.

Flat land to hills and cliffs

The Yangtze Princess went through the locks today allowing us to enter the three gorges. A drizzle was falling, and the ship was behind schedule. By the time we arrived at the Three Gorges Dam construction site it was too dark to see much. The current was quite swift. The ship channel was winding. At times, the channel ran very close to the rocky mountainous shore. As darkness fell, three strong searchlights were turned on and played on the rocks and the river. Progress against the current was slow. There are stretches along the river where traffic is one-way. Permission must be received before such a section can be transited. Here I saw for the first-time traces of the old path carved from solid stone the path used by coolies to pull the ship upstream. Our guide said there are still some sections in the smaller side gorges where coolies still are employed for this purpose.

Fish Research Institute

We visited a fish research institute today. The primary goal of the institute is to find a way to preserve the Chinese Sturgeon. The Three Gorges Dam will cut off the route to their spawning area. The Institute is trying to develop an artificial breeding area. We were shown a video claiming that they are succeeding in this effort. I had my doubts but did not express them. It seems that my doubts have been confirmed by the research below.

The sturgeon is found only in the middle and lower Yangtze River and close to the shores in the East China Sea and the Yellow Sea.[xvii]

Xinhua reported[1] that no wild sturgeon reproduced naturally last year in the Yangtze River.

---

1.   http://www.zj.xinhuanet.com/newscenter/rb/2014-09/14/c_1112470401.htm

It was the first time since researchers began recording levels 32 years ago.

Chinese research says the fall is due to rising levels of pollution in the Yangtze River and the construction of dozens of dams.

Researchers from the Chinese Academy of Fishery Sciences also found that no young sturgeons were found swimming along the Yangtze toward the sea during the period they usually do so.

A researcher told Xinhua that in the 1980s, at least several thousand sturgeons could be found in the river. It is estimated only around 100 fish remain.

"Without natural reproduction, the fish population cannot replenish itself. If there are no further steps taken to strengthen conservation, the wild sturgeon faces the danger of extinction," he said.[xviii]

Waterfalls were always in sight. Some fell long distances, others did not. In the canyon cut by the river many waterfalls fell from the top to the base of the cliff. October was past the summer rainy season. Many of the waterfalls must have been roaring during the wet season. I always enjoy watching waterfalls.

Chongqing

First Sight

I woke up early. Today I would be in Chongqing. Sitting up in my bed, I pulled the curtains back so I could peek out the window. Below me the muddy waters rolled by. Clouds hung low and a gentle rain fell making little rings in the water as drops hit. On the shore I could see the green of winter vegetables. Placing my hand on the windowpane I could tell it was a cool morning. We were not yet in Chongqing, but if we arrived on schedule, I would be there in two to three hours.

After washing and shaving, I went out on deck standing in the lee of a wall that protected me from the rain. I stood trying to imagine how it must have appeared when a sortie of Japanese bombers and fighters streaked down the Yangtze to bomb the city. Where did the spotters watch for the planes? How much notice did Chongqing receive? Was there any opposition rising to greet the intruder planes with the big red meatball painted on their wings?

Later I learned that when the planes were 30 minutes away from Chongqing, men released a tethered balloon giving warning of an impending bombing. At 15 minutes out a second balloon was released. By the time the third balloon went up, bombs were already falling.

As we approached Chongqing, I saw steps leading to the city from a ferry landing. The steps showed me how I was to navigate getting to the city above the river. There was no pier, no dock. The ship stopped out in the river, beside a long narrow boardwalk that ran to the rocky shore. I pulled my backpack up onto my shoulders and made my way to the exit, out the door, down a short ramp and onto the rain slick boardwalk. The current was quite swift at this point. Porters, some half naked, came running hoping to make few "kwai" carrying the traveler's bags. Ignoring me, they had no hope in a foreigner who had only a backpack; they rushed past toward fellow suitcase-lugging travelers.

Waiting for the ferry

The rain had lessened into a cold drizzle ... just enough to keep the boardwalk slick. At the end of the boardwalk, I had no choice but to pick my way through the mud and river rocks to a stairway leading up a fifty-foot-high rock cliff to the city streets. The ancient wet stone steps were worn so each step was inclined outward making footing difficult at best. To my dismay mud and water covered the steps making them slick as ice. "Heavens," I thought, "easy to break a leg here. I'd better be careful. I really do not need a broken leg at this point in my life!"

I carefully made my way up the steep, wet, muddy, slippery set of stone stairs to the city built on bare granite mountains above. As I climbed, porters swept past me running down the stairs. Beggars called out, holding 'praying hands' together, moving them up and down, the same movement that people made praying at Buddhist temples. At the top of the stairs, street vendors spread trinkets, cigarettes, Chinese medicine, and other goods on blankets lying on the street. Beggars and vendors called me as I walked past. By now, I had become adept at ignoring both by never looking their way. I knew with one look in their direction their shouting would raise in volume and the more aggressive vendors would grab an item and walk my way holding it out for inspection shouting "Look, look," "cheap, cheap" or "hello, hello."

Winded and legs hurting from the climb, I was ready for my next task, finding a taxi and traveling to Chongqing University. In just over a week, I had traveled by train from Xi'an to Wuhan and then by riverboat up the Yangtze River to Chongqing. Tomorrow I was to go to my ultimate destination the remote city of Guizhou, the capital of Guiyang, an 18-hour trip by train from Chongqing.

Honest Taxi Driver

I had no idea how far I was from the university, but I was not worried. A friend in Xi'an had written a note for me to show the taxi driver telling her where I wanted to go. He had told me how much the fare should be if the driver was honest. Honest taxi drivers were an iffy thing in a Chinese city in 1995.

I looked around but saw no taxi. A parked tour bus waited. That was of no interest to me. Puzzled I wondered which way I should walk. To my left there was a long sloping street leading to an open square. Hoping for a taxi stand, I walked down the incline. Entering the square, I saw many cars parked and a yellow taxicab at the far side of the square. I waved my hand. The driver, a woman, saw me and motioned for me to come and get in the taxi. As I neared the taxi, I asked using my best Chinese, "Nǐ huì shuō yīngyǔ ma?" [Do you speak English?]

"Bù, wǒ", [No] she replied with a smile and a shrug of her shoulders.

I pulled a small notebook out of my backpack and flipped through the pages until I found the note that read, "Please take this foreigner to the Foreign Affairs Office at Chongqing University. He has spent the summer working at Northwestern Polytechnical University in Xi'an and is touring China." I handed her the notebook.

Shaking her head as if saying, 'Oh yes,' she read the note, flashed a smile, and giving me a thumbs up she popped the clutch, and off we went through a city that was all up and down. There are no flat places in Chongqing. Steps cut into the granite mountainsides ran up from the street, disappearing in the distant heights. A friend in Xi'an told me, "There are no bicycles in Chongqing". Now I knew why. In Chongqing, people walk on the sidewalks and in turn climb and descend the stone staircases. Men carrying huge loads weighing hundreds of pounds suspended on bamboo pools. Once, I saw four men carrying an industrial-size electric motor. It was tied to two bamboo poles, each at least eight inches in diameter and seven feet long. This was the first time I saw the bent knees and shuffling trot of men carrying heavy loads suspended from bamboo poles.

Chongqing University

Entering Chongqing University forty minutes later the driver stopped in front of a tall building. Glancing at the meter, I saw the fare was almost exactly what my friend in Xi'an said it should be. Relieved and a bit surprised at her honesty. I paid the 32 kwai fare and gave her an 8 kwai tip, about one dollar. I had eaten two meals a day at street-side restaurants for that amount, so it was a good tip.

The lady taxi driver counted the money gave me a big smile and a double xiè xiè, [thank you]. She pointed to the building's main door, and shook her finger, letting me know that is where I needed to go. I said goodbye to her as I closed the door and watched her make a U-turn and head back to the city.

I entered the building wondering how I was to find the Foreign Affairs Office. I need not have wondered. Just ahead to my left was an open door. Walking to the door I saw two young men sitting and talking. Immediately, they stood when they saw me and asked, "Are you Bill Lively?"

"Yes," I replied as we shook hands.

"Good, we have been expecting you. Mr. Zhou will take you to the university guest house. The registration forms were already filled out.

Two people were waiting for me. This surprised me. It was Saturday, a day off for most people. I suspected one was sitting with a friend, helping the time pass until the foreigner showed up.

Mr. Zhou turned to me, "I'll show you the way to the guesthouse. It is quite a long walk. Our campus is long and narrow."

He was right. We walked at least a mile before arriving at the guesthouse. Finding it on my own would have been difficult, not impossible but difficult.

As we walked, I asked him, "How much will the room cost? When I leave tomorrow, most people will be away, and the desk clerk may not speak English."

Mr. Zhou thought a few seconds before replying. "There is no charge."

"Why is that?" I responded. "I have expected to pay."

"Well," he replied, "it's not a very nice room.

Laughing I replied, "That is a very good price."

Now he was laughing. "I will show you where the desk clerk will be and explain it to her."

At the guesthouse, we checked in and he led me to a second-floor room. Entering the room, I saw that the carpet and wallpaper had seen much better days. The torn and thread-bare carpet spoke of years of use and smelled of mildew. Tears and stains on the wallpaper showed their age. The bathroom had an Asian toilet, a ceramic-lined hole in the floor, a sink, and a bathtub. During the years of use the white bathtub had turned rust colored red. There was a shower head, but no curtain. I immediately made the decision that I would squat in the tub to shower to avoid spraying water all over the room. On the plus side, the room had a new air-conditioner and, though this was October, the warmth and humidity made the day uncomfortable. Also, there was a new TV which meant little to me as my Chinese was poor to say the least. The best attribute of the room was the pillow, sheets and covers on the twin bed were new and sparkling clean. Give me a clean bed and the rest is secondary.

"This is great," I said. "Tomorrow, where can I catch a taxi?

He answered, "Just outside the back gate. It is to the right of the hotel door. Just stand at the gate and flag the first taxi. They come by often. I must go now."

He paused and then asked, "Would you like to teach here next year? We have several openings for English teachers."

" I appreciate the offer," I said. "But I have to go home at the end of this month."

"Well," he said, "if you meet anyone looking for a job let me know."

I told him I would. We shook hands and he left.

At lunch, I met a young man who was teaching that year. He told me that several people who had agreed to teach backed out in late July and the university had not been able to replace them.

"How is it going for you?" I was curious.

"Well," he sighed, "I am working twenty hours a week instead of the fourteen I was promised, but I like the university and my classes. What I do not like is the heat and humidity here."

I laughed, "A Chinese friend told me that Chongqing is one of the four furnaces of China. It has a reputation for being uncomfortable."

Pigeons

I looked out my window across a steep valley. As I looked, I saw a man walk onto the roof of an apartment building and go toward a structure. He opened a door, and several dozen pigeons flew out, up and over the city. For several minutes they flew in circles and then settled back into their home. I could not determine how he communicated with his birds, but I was sure he did. During the day I watched him exercise his pigeons several times.

As I was watching the pigeons during one of their exercise periods, I looked to my left. Several windows down a cat was lying on an air conditioner. This in itself was not noteworthy. However, there was a straight-down drop of over two hundred feet off the AC. Though cats have a good sense of balance it seemed to me that this cat was putting one of its nine lives in jeopardy.

Train Ticket

Zhou, from the Waiban, walked to the guest house and handed me an envelope. "Here is your train ticket to Guiyang," I thanked him, opened the envelope, took the ticket out, and was surprised that the charge was the foreign teacher's fare. This was considerably lower than the regular fare I expected to pay. The fare was ¥138 or about $17.25. The regular fare was ¥194 or about $24.95 for hard sleeper. There were no soft sleeper cars.

I said, "Zhou, I do not have a teacher's card with me. Will that cause me a problem?"

Smiling he said, "I will write a note for you. Show it to anyone who asks you about why you paid as a foreign teacher. I will write something for you." Saying this he pulled a small notebook out of his attaché case.

"Here, don't use yours," I said, "write in my notebook. I will always have it with me."

Taking my notebook, he turned to a blank page. In Chinese, he wrote, "Please help this foreigner, Bill Lively. He has spent the summer teaching at the Northwestern Polytechnic University. Now he is touring China. In his excitement about leaving, he forgot his teacher ID card. Thank you." Telling the truth in such situations never seemed a high priority in 1995 China.

I gave him the money for the train ticket and thanked him for the help he had given me. We shook hands and said goodbye to each other. As he left, I put the note and the ticket into the envelope and zipped it into a secure pocket of my journalist jacket.

It was hours before I needed to catch a taxi to the station. Regardless, I decided to check out of the room and catch a cab. Chongqing is a huge city, and I did not want to wait and risk the possibility of a traffic jam or accident and arriving late. Once I was sure I had secured everything in various pockets and my backpack was filled, I made my way to the front desk and turned in the room key. Smiling the desk clerk, a young woman, thanked me in Chinese. Leaving the guest house, I was on my way to remote Guizhou.

Taxi to the Train Station

I stood just outside the back gate of the Chongqing University waiting to catch a taxi. Zhou's information on taxis was right when he said my wait would not be more than a few minutes. In just two or three minutes a taxi drove up, two passengers got out. They looked like professors to me. The driver waved me in.

Climbing in on the passenger side, I showed the driver the note saying I wanted to go to the train station. Shaking his head, he pushed the arm on the timer/fare machine on the dashboard and off we went. I watched the city and granite mountainsides roll past. Again, I saw the cut stone steps going straight up until they disappeared. Many appeared worn, like those I climbed from the river. Traffic was heavy but moved well.

Waiting at the Train Station

Thirty minutes later the taxi pulled into the large slick muddy water covered square in front of the train station. I paid the driver and thanked him. A light rain was falling turning dust into a thin layer of mud. The mud and tiny rocks covered the cobblestones. Taxi cabs waited for travelers coming out of the station. Only a few people were in the square, the rain having chased most folk inside. Peasants sat outside under the cover of a roof, talking, staring ahead, and sleeping. It is the same at every rail station I visited while in China. Patiently they wait. My feeling is that when not working on their plots of land much of their life is spent waiting. They never block the entrance. A few of the peasants had small suitcases. I saw no umbrellas or raincoats. Most had woven plastic bags that were colorful, strong and in all sizes, from small to large enough to hold all my clothes as well as Nancy's at home in Annapolis.

After paying the driver, I entered the station. To my left was a small magazine stand with an open space beyond. To my right three or four ticket booths stood with a line of people at each one. Directly ahead of me I saw a large waiting area. I was sure a thousand or more people could be in the room; not all sitting but waiting in the room. Ahead of me was a long railing with turnstiles in the center. The only entrance to the waiting area was the turnstile. The rail and turnstile separated the waiting area for the ticketing area. Overhead hung a large arrivals and departure board. Whenever information changed, was removed, or added, there was rapid clicking as the letters and numbers changed.

The Waiting Area

At the turnstile two young women stood, wearing railroad worker uniforms. They were the ticket checkers. "Should I show them my note?" I asked myself. "Would that be stupid or wise?" I pondered the question. "If the ticket is a problem, it is best to find out now while there was time for any problem to be solved. If there is no problem, perhaps it is best to, 'let a sleeping dog lay.'" Finally, I decided I'd best show them my note. "Good news will let me sit easy. Bad news, I still have time to correct the problem."

I walked across the room. The young women watched me walking toward them and began giggling. I could imagine them thinking, "Oh no, here comes an 'old' American and he is going to ask us a question."

Using my best Chinese, I said, "Ni hao" "Hello," and held out the notebook opened to the page containing of Zhou's message. Giggling one simply turned and walked away. I did not consider her impolite. I took it to mean she simply did not want to have to deal with a foreigner. I did not blame her. The brave one took the notebook and read.

Looking at me she handed me the notebook and motioned for me to stand still. Turning, she walked away. Now what I wondered to do but wait. A few minutes later she returned with an older man. I assumed he was her supervisor though I never knew that for a fact. I also assumed he spoke English though he never spoke at all in either Chinese or English. I handed him the notebook and my ticket. He read the note and looked at the ticket. Without a word he took my elbow, as I would a small child, and led me through the turnstile into the waiting area. He then returned my notebook and ticket. Once we were in the waiting area, he flicked his wrist and pointed to his watch and at a seat. His meaning was clear, "SIT DOWN AND DON'T MOVE." I sat down. Satisfied, he walked away. That was the last I saw of him. I never saw the two women again. Hours later when we boarded the train, they were off work and probably home.

I set my backpack between my feet. I pulled out the ticket and read train K9517 car number 6, bunk 23. Why is it that I felt the need to check the ticket, as I already knew what it said? Now I had a long wait. I was alone in the waiting area with lots of time to read, nap or just sit and watch the whirl of activity. Alone in a big room is a surreal experience in China. Normally there is standing room only in train stations. As shown later this became true here.

Looking around I cased the room. Rows of hard, wooden benches provided seating. Long-tubed buzzing fluorescent lights chased the gloom away. At the far end of the room, thirty or more feet away, another rail channeled the travelers to three small gates showing the way to the train platforms. Looking around I saw a sign for toilets on one side.

In China there are three classes of service on trains: the soft sleeper, hard-sleeper, and hard seat. Soft sleeper is a compartment with four soft bunks: hard sleeper with sleeping boards five high covered with thick brown high plastic. Hard seat is exactly that, hard wooden seats facing each other with a wooden picnic type table between. They are much less expensive.

My earlier travels had always been in soft sleeper. Soft sleeper waiting rooms are small. They have overstuffed chairs for comfort, plus there is a bit of privacy. Hard-sleeper rooms are large. The seats are wooden, hard, and filled, with an overflow of people sitting, standing, lying on the floor in any available space.

An hour passed. A few people came into the room. Another hour passed and now the room was filling rapidly. People arrived in ones, twos and in family groups, carrying all manner of boxes, bags, packages, and suitcases. Picking seats, they also began their vigil. The sound of the buzzing fluorescent lights soon disappeared in a rising crescendo of voices. No one approached to practice his or her English.

A young man, his wife, and child sat next to me. Soon the little boy was fast asleep on the soft cloth travel bag sitting on the floor. They were talking quietly; it was as if they were alone. I wondered how far they would travel. There were four stops between Chongqing and Guiyang. Poverty is great in Guizhou Provence. Harrison Salisbury in his book, *The Long March* wrote that when Mao and the Red Army passed through Guizhou, they were shocked at the poverty. Though poverty was great in China they had never seen such poverty as that which greeted them in Guizhou. In 1995 it was still one of the poorest provinces in China.

"Hard sleeper will be an interesting experience," I thought. "I'll be with 'real' Chinese, not party officials, military officers, traveling professors, and 'rich' Chinese."

Slowly the hours of waiting dragged on. I read; I watched people; taking my backpack with me I paid an attendant and used the restroom.

Slowly the minutes went by. The room continued to fill until it seemed there was no room for another person. People were standing, sitting, lying on their belongings, squatting, reading, writing, talking, eating, sewing and many squatted simply absently staring ahead. Travelers can eat, but not smoke. Women open bags of sunflower seeds. With an ability I never achieved, they split them with their front teeth, spit out the shells and eat the nut inside. Spitting is not taboo in China. There was nothing for me to do but wait and wait and wait. I was not bored. It was fascinating people watching. By boarding time, the room was crammed with people, sitting, standing, and squatting. Numerous children were laying on their parent's plastic bags sleeping. Adults were reading, some were talking, some were dozing and many simply sat staring ahead.

Night Train to Guizhou

I was traveling to Guiyang, the capital of Guizhou province to visit the parents of Hai, a student at St. John's College in Annapolis. Nancy and I lived within walking distance of the college and Hai lived with us during three of his four years there.

The digital clock on the arrivals/departures board clicked off the minutes. Suddenly as the clock clicked from 10:29 to 10:30 a murmur rose in the waiting area. People began gathering up their standing, stretching, waking kids, yawning, putting items in their traveling bags, boxes, and suitcases. It did not take much male intuition to know the check-in process was about to begin. It was time for me to join the action. I knew that when the turnstiles opened it would be like a floodgate opening. Three young railway workers took their places at the turnstiles.

Four rows of wooden benches created three aisles. This channeled passengers to turnstiles as the far end of the room. This forced people to stay in one area and created a bit of order in what could have been chaos.

Tightly packed

Picking up my backpack I joined the crowd gathering at the turnstile. I was ten or so feet back. Everyone stood massed together, tightly packed. Behind me, some poor soul was jammed against me. His or her head pushed between my shoulder blades. I had to lean back to avoid putting even more pressure on the person ahead of me. The thought came to me that I could have a heart attack, die, and not fall to the floor. The crush of people would hold me upright, at least until we parted at the turnstile. It was like waiting for a bus, butt to belly, belly to butt.

With itty-bitty steps, I moved toward the turnstile. Ten or so minutes later I was there. Here was the next to last test. Would the young woman, who punched the tickets, ask to see my Teacher ID Card? I hoped ... no, I prayed she would not. Finally, I was face to face with her. I handed her my ticket. Quickly she glanced at it, punched it and handed it back to me. Deftly she motioned me through. One test down and one more to go, then I can breathe easy. One prayer answered.

I did not know how far it was to the train. That was not a worry. All I had to do was follow the crowd. They were experienced. They knew what they were doing. At least that was my assumption. There were those who ran to the train. I had seen people at other stations run to a hard-sleeper car and with the help of others already aboard be pulled through an open window. Hard-sleeper seats are not reserved resulting in a first come, first served. I pitied those who arrived late and could not find a seat as they could only stand until a seat became available at a stop down the road. A friend told me that as a student on the way home during a holiday he had to stand holding his overnight case over his head for three hours. The car was so crowded he could not lower his hands.

I followed others down a poorly lit passageway, then down a long set of steps to a platform. To my left was the train, a long line of green cars with yellow stripes. Car number 17 stood beside the platform at the bottom of the stairs. My ticket was for car number 6. Thus, I had a long walk ahead of me. Looking through the windows of each car as I walked, I saw hard seat car, hard seat car, hard seat car, hard seat car, hard seat car, baggage car, dining car, hard seat car, hard seat car. Passing car 10 I looked ahead. "Gee," I thought, "I'm going to run out of platform before I get to number 6. Passing car 10 I saw that 9 was a hard sleeper. Car 8 was another hard sleeper. Passing 8 I saw the next car was the last car beside the platform. To my surprise, it carried the number 6. I had no idea where car 7 was or if there was a car 7. Does this have something to do with Chinese numerology? I know the number 4 is an unlucky number as its pronunciation is close to the pronunciation of death or dead. Is 7 an unlucky number? I found it is. Seven (◇qu) is an odd number, a yang number. Its pronunciation is close to the word for gone and relates to ceremonies that release dead souls from purgatory. Also, the pronouncement is close to that of deceive.[xix] Death and deceived, both are negative words.

The Last and Acid Test

A young woman, the car's attendant, stood on the platform at the door. Here was the last test, the acid test, the go home or go to jail test. I could feel a small lump of anxiety beginning to build in my stomach. One of my little philosophies of life is when you don't know what you are doing, act like you do know what you are doing. Showing false confidence goes much further than showing real anxiety.

Walking forward with a smile ... Americans always smile you know ... I handed her my ticket. Quickly she opened a leather case and removed a metal tag. After handing me the tag she carefully folded my ticket and slid it in one of the slots in her case. Shortly before arriving at Guiyang, she would collect the tag and return my ticket. To exit the station, I'd have to show my ticket at the exit turnstile.

With a feeling of relief, I climbed the three steps into the car. An aisle ran down the right side of the car. Steel poles with three bunks attached on each side ran the length of the car. I made my way down an aisle looking for number 23, my bunk. Seeing it I checked my tag to be sure the number 23 was stamped into the metal. I was happy to note it was a middle bunk. Friends had told me that the middle bunk is best. People like to gather together, sit on the lower bunk and talk. The upper bunk is high and difficult to get in and out of without bothering those below. Like the chair, porridge, and bed in Goldilocks, the middle bunk is just right.

Hard Sleeper

Hard sleeper

Hard sleeper was an open car with an aisle running the length of the car on one side. The other side would hold 90 to 99 passengers in triple bunks.

Two sparkling white sheets, one covering the plastic pad and one that served as a top sheet greeted me. A small pillow with a shining white pillowcase lay at the end of the bunk away from the aisle. Under the pillow, a blue cover lay folded. I stowed my backpack on the ledge, and climbed into bunk number 23, a middle bunk, and settled in for the night of "hard sleeper" rest. As I settled in, I noticed two leather straps attached to the upper bunk. Each had an attachment. Looking down I saw there was a place to attach the straps. This was a safety harness to keep me from rolling out and falling to the floor if the train made a sudden stop or I, on my own, fell out of bed.

There is an unwritten rule in the Chinese culture; when on a train, other passengers' belongings are not to be touched. The fully packed luggage rack ran along one side of the car. Personal belongings, woven plastic bags and small suitcases filled every inch of space. No one showed any apprehension or concern that their belongings would be bothered and in all my travels in China I never saw this rule violated.

Three or four men sat on the two bottom bunks chatting. Other travelers stowed their belongings and settled into their bunks for the night. I did not notice any kids in the car. Were they all in the hard seat car? I'll never know. Stowing my shoes at the head of my bunk I pulled up the cover and lay down to sleep. I thought the chatting men might bother me, but in ten minutes or so they parted. By now the train was moving. I snapped the harness together. By now the train was on its way, the car rocking gently. Soon everyone had settled in and except for the click-clack of the rails all was quiet and I fell asleep.

Guiyang, Guizhou[XX]

Approaching Guiyang

I woke as the glow from the sun grew in intensity inside the hard-sleeper car. Eager to see the countryside I climbed out of my bunk, put on my shoes, went to the toilet – thank goodness it was an Eastern toilet.[xxi] Surprisingly no one was in the toilet, no waiting line. Once back at my bunk I stood in the aisle watching the countryside roll past. There was little for me to see as trees grew close to the train tracks obscuring views into the distance. Even with a limited view, I could see this was a mountainous area.

I glanced at my watch and was surprised; we were only twenty minutes out of Guizhou provided we arrived on schedule. The train entered a long tunnel. Exiting the tunnel, we entered the outskirts of the city. In another ten minutes the train slowed to a stop at the station. A familiar scene followed; thousands, or so it seemed, of people poured out of the train onto the platform. Slowly I followed the people in front of me to the door of the car. Stepping down, I joined those already on the crowded platform. I was not worried. I knew that someone from Hai's family would meet me, but I did not know if they would meet me on the platform or in the station. Guiyang is remote and   as   far   as   I   saw   I   was   the   only

Sun Hai's parents

pale, white foreigner on the train. Indeed, in the week I spent in Guiyang, I saw only one other foreigner. I was a minority of one.

I slowly made my way along the platform toward the exit. The crowd whirled around me. Suddenly I saw a familiar face. I had met Hai's parents who stayed in our home in Annapolis during the time of Hai's undergraduate graduation. It was Hai's mother. Our eyes met and a smile spread across her face. I smiled back, happy to see her. When traveling in a foreign country it is always good to see the friendly face of a person waiting for you. I walked to her and shook her hand. Immediately Hai's father joined us, he was also smiling.

They were surprised I did not have a suitcase; I only had a backpack and my travel vest. Pack light, travel light was my motto.

We made our way out of the station. I knew from a map I had received in Xi'an that their apartment was near the station. I also knew our verbal communications would be limited. My Chinese was poor, and my host's English matched my Chinese. I wondered if we would walk to their apartment; take a bus or a taxi. Now I was in their hands. They were my guardians and guides.

We walked outside. Hai's father hailed a taxi. We climbed in and off we went arriving almost before I had time to settle my backpack between my feet.

The morning was bright and sunny. The air was clear. Bright sunshine and clear air, what a novelty in China where air pollution is so heavy. In other cities the sky was seldom blue. The temperature here was 75F, wonderfully comfortable. Guiyang is almost always comfortable and is called the 2nd city of eternal spring; a city where it is never too cold or too hot. Kunming is the 1st city of eternal spring.

Stepping stones

They gave me a tour of the downtown area, where they lived before moving, and Hai's high school. Later we went to a city park. There is a river running through the park. Steppingstones allow a person to cross the river. This is where I thought of the idea of steppingstones in writing as a theme for this memoir.

Harvesting Rice

The Guizhou area is landlocked and mountainous. For centuries there was no ready access to the outside world. It was a hard scrabble rice farming existence. To me in 1995 peasants in Guizhou looked more impoverished than beggars I had seen in Xi'an and other cities in China. During their Long March before 1946, Mao and others were shocked and amazed at the poverty. It was worse than they had seen in the cities and countryside in other places.

One of Hai's uncles owned a Volkswagen Golf. The family had decided to treat me to a nice visit to a famous area of China and we were on our way. The drive was mostly through rural areas. We were on our way to the largest waterfall in China, Huangguoshu. Dragon teeth mountains were everywhere. Each stood alone. Between the mountains golden rice was being harvested. At the base of many of the mountains were graves. I had never seen this before.

In the fields peasants bent over and cut the rice growing there with sickles then dropped it onto the ground. Others would gather the rice, stems and all, and carry it to a large wooden box-shaped structure. The sides of the box were inclined, larger at the top, smaller at the bottom. I looked ahead and saw one of the containers near the road. A woman stood on each side beating the rice against the inside of the box. As they beat the grains of rice came loose.

As we approached, I saw one woman was elderly, two middle-aged, and one was young and beautiful. They were talking as they worked. Just as we were passing, one must have said something funny. The young woman looked up, laughing. I wondered how long her beauty would last working threshing rice in the sun. This was a hard life she was living. Living in a poor province with little or no chance for education left her with no choice but to work hard and hope she could grow enough food to not go hungry. The Chinese greeting for a good morning is, "Have you eaten today?" I hoped this young woman would always answer, "Yes."

We drove through another area where a minority group lives and builds their houses and roofs of stone. In 2000 Nancy and I were told that Western 'experts' believed before seeing these houses that such multiple story buildings were impossible to build. They were wrong. In several hours we were at the Huangguoshu.

A narrow path crossed a steep hillside above the river to the left edge of the waterfall. From there the path crossed behind the falling water exiting on the right side of the falls. Crossing behind the falling water was not without danger as it was pitch dark. I had to slowly feel my way. The roar of the falling water filled my ears, but it was fun, even though there was some danger of tripping over invisible rocks. The path continued to a swinging bridge which we crossed to return to the car. I was in Guizhou for a week and saw no Westerners except at Huangguoshu. There I saw one other Westerner, only one.

Guiyang to Xi'an

To return to Xi'an from Guiyang I had a choice, either by rail or by air. By rail it was a two-day trip, first from Guiyang to Chongqing to Chengdu and finally to Xi'an. I did not want to spend two days on a train. Also, at that time I would have had to buy a ticket from Guiyang to Chongqing. In Chongqing I would have had to buy a ticket from there to Chengdu and finally in Chengdu I would have had to buy a ticket to Xi'an. It was impossible, at that time, to buy a ticket from one city to the destination if there was a major city between the origin and terminus of the trip. At times it was not possible to buy a ticket for the same day and a trip might be delayed for days until a ticket was available. It was difficult for an independent foreign traveler to negotiate this arcane system.

The flight from Guiyang to Xi'an was a ninety-minute flight. With Hai's parents' help, purchasing a ticket did not present a problem. The solution was simple. I would travel by air.

Day of flight

I walked across the tarmac with others and boarded the airplane, a new Boeing 737. By the time everyone was aboard, the plane was full. There were five flight attendants to serve us. Announcements were made in Chinese and English. The use of the oxygen masks was demonstrated but not of using the seat belt. As far as I knew, I was the only foreigner aboard. I was pleased when the announcement was made that no smoking was allowed during the flight. Most Chinese men smoke and I had feared smoking would be allowed, and the passenger area would become thick with cigarette smoke.

Contrast

As the plane turned at the end of the runway, I looked out the window. Not more than one hundred yards from me was a stone wall. Just beyond the stone wall, a peasant was hoeing the ground. What a contrast! He was using a tool that had been used for hundreds of years, for generation upon generation before him. If he had worn the clothing of his ancestors, there would have been nothing showing he lived in the twentieth century. I was sitting on a new Boeing 737 filled with the latest electronic equipment. Could our worlds have been any more different than this?

Flight

The plane lifted off the runway and I watched the earth pass under me. Many of the hills were terraced, some to the top. This was not apparent from ground level. The rice paddies highlighted the level land between the hills and mountains. The golden rice paddies and green hills were a beautiful contrast, appearing like a mosaic below me.

The clouds over Guizhou were puffy and white. As we approached Xi'an, they thickened and obscured the landscape. My guess was the plane broke out of the clouds at about fifteen hundred feet. The landing was smooth. For this I was thankful.

I exited the airplane and walked across the tarmac before entering the terminal. Liu Shengwu was there. As we greeted each other, I realized I had left a small notebook in the pocket ahead of my seat.

"I have to return to the plane," I said.

"Why," he asked.

"I left a small notebook in the seat pocket. It has a lot of notes and for me it would be a sad loss."

"I'll wait for you," he said.

I was surprised as no one challenged me as I exited the door and returned to the plane. Three or four young men in military uniforms stood near the plane. A stewardess was walking down the ramp.

"Excuse me," I said as I motioned to her. "I left a small notebook in the pocket ahead of my seat."

Smiling she asked, "What was your seat number?"

I told her. She turned and climbed up the steps and entered the airplane.

One of the uniformed men walked up to me. "What is it you want?" he asked.

I explained, telling him the stewardess was getting it for me. Just then she exited the plane and walked down the rampway. When she reached me, she handed me my notebook. I thanked her and returned to the terminal.

Liu Shengwu and I returned to NPU by bus where I checked into the guesthouse. After checking in, Shengwu took me to his apartment for our evening meal.

Tomb of the Yellow Emperor

It was late in October, and I had only a few days left before heading home. Qian Fupei and Liu Shengwu asked me if I would like to visit the tomb of the Yellow Emperor. My thought was, why not? I had nothing of importance I needed to do. "Sure," I replied.

Supposedly born in 2704 BC, the Yellow Emperor is a mythical figure. Knowing this I was skeptical there was such a tomb. Regardless, I thought it would be an interesting day trip as we would drive 145 miles from Xi'an into northern Shaanxi, an area I had never seen. I would have liked to visit Yan'an where Mao and the Red Army stayed during the war against Japan. However, it was 198 miles from Xi'an, too far on the roads at that time for a day trip.

Either Fupei or Shengwu reserved a university van. In the morning, Fupei, his wife, Yeying, Shengwu and two young women from Fupei's department, and I climbed into the van and off we went. The driver was cautious once we were out of Xi'an. It was a cold, wet, and foggy day. The loess soil, when wet, is slippery like ice. Thus, if there was any loess soil on the road, then the narrow two-laned roads would be slick. Soon, we were climbing into the hills and mountains. The first hills were terraced from top to bottom. The terrace walls varied from two feet to five or six feet in height. The green of winter wheat colored the fields. As we travelled north, the hills became steeper and higher and finally turned into mountains covered with scrub brush. My feeling was that if trees could be planted, in several decades the mountains would be forest covered.

Numerous coal trucks drove in both directions. Those going north were empty. Those going south were filled with coal. A three- or four-foot ditch ran along each side of the road. As we drove, I saw three or four trucks turned on their side into the ditch. Also, at intervals sat trucks which had broken down. Some had flat tires. Others had broken axles, and I could not identify the problem with others that sat still on the highway. My guess was that preventative maintenance was not a high priority and the result was the silently sitting trucks. I guessed the philosophy was, drive it until it breaks, fix it where it breaks. To me, this was a pound-wise and penny-foolish philosophy. This reminded me of something I saw while riding a train from Xi'an to Beijing in 1992. It was early in the morning. The train was going through mountains east of Taiyuan in Shanxi Province. I stood in the aisleway looking out. Across a steep valley was a narrow road winding up into the mountains. We came to a place where I saw a coal truck broken down on the road. As far as I could see, there were trucks, blocked by the kaput one. For miles there was a line of trucks which could not move further. The line of stalled trucks continued until the road turned and disappeared behind a mountain. There must have been over a thousand none of which were going anywhere. "What a waste" I thought.

It took about four hours before we arrived at the Yellow King's Tomb located on top a hill. A town was nearby but we did not go there. There was not much to see. The day was so dark that without a flash I could not take any photos. I wondered if anyone was buried here. To me the most impressive sight was a grove of huge cypress trees. I had never seen such a grove in China, and I wondered how it had survived. Was this spot so remote that the Red Guards in the Cultural Revolution never came here? Was it remote enough that peasants never came to cut the trees? I asked but no one in the group had an answer. Fortunately, there was a concrete walkway to the tomb else the walk to and from the location would have presented a real danger of slipping and falling. The soil here was also that slippery loess variety.

Our return to NPU went smoothly. We made a stop somewhere in the mountains at a roadside restaurant for a meal. By 6:00 pm we were back at the university. After eating supper with Fupei and Yeying, I returned to the guesthouse and called it a day.

Visa Problem

Visa Defined

A visa is a legal agreement from a government allowing a person to enter the country. Some are single entry visas and others are multi-entry. Regardless, all visas are granted for a given period of time. This can be short, a few days, too long, a few years. I believe the visa I received from the Chilean government was multiple entry for ten years.

I was in my room at the guest house of NPU. Only a month was left before I was to fly home when I began thinking of my return to the States. My ticket was for October 31st. I knew my visa was for 180 days. My entry into China had been on May 2nd. October 31st was more than 180 days, and this meant I had a problem. To double check, I pulled my calendar out of a desk drawer and began counting. I counted once. I counted twice. I counted a third time. Each count ended with the 180th day being October 29th, two days before I was to leave China. Scratching my head, I thought, "Now what? How do I get an extension? Is it possible? Should I just go to the airport and hope Customs does not notice? I rejected that idea quickly. Not only did that seem unwise. It seemed stupid. I decided that I should look at this calmly and rationally. Immediately I thought I could get help at the university Foreign Affairs Office and Zheng Qian and Xiao Lei. Surely my problem was not unique. Surely this little problem had come up before. I would go there and get their advice.

The next morning, I walked to the Foreign Affairs Office. Xiao Lei welcomed me into his office. I explained my problem. "Yes," he said, "we will go to the Security Police, and they should be able to help you. I'll call them and make an appointment. I'll let you know when we can go ... it will be in a day or two."

Security Police

On the day of the appointment, we took a taxi to the office of the Security police located in the ancient part of the city, inside the Ming Wall. The Security police's office was on West Street.

We entered the office. There was a small waiting area with a desk on one side of a counter. Xiao Lei exchanged greetings with two police officers seated behind a counter. My impression was they knew each other. As the conversation was in Chinese, I had no clue what they were saying. I took it as a good sign that the conversation remained cordial, calm with no raised voices. This continued for two to three minutes. Then Xian Lei turned to me, "They say that 'yes', they can extend your visa here, but it would be better if you did so in Tianjin. Here it will take several weeks. The university will have to write a letter for you. They will have to send everything to higher authorities and wait for their reply. If you go to the Security police in Tianjin, it should take about ten minutes."

This seemed strange to me, but my experience in China had taught me that nothing is straight forward. Laws and procedures, if you can call them that, seemed to vary from place to place. For instance, postage rates for my letters to the States varied from city to city. It seemed to me that the 'law' was whatever the bureaucrat on the other side of the counter decided that day.

I thought for a moment deciding what to do next. Either they are telling me the truth, or they simply do not want to be bothered. Regardless I decided it would be unwise to pursue the extension in Xi'an. The Security police, if they were not telling the truth, could certainly delay the process and could reject the application for any or no reason. "O.K., thank them for their help. I'll have my friend Li Zhi help me in Tianjin".

We all smiled and shook hands. Xiao Lei and I returned to NPU.

Xiao Lei, from the Foreign Affairs Office, gave me my train ticket to travel from Xi'an to Tianjin, leaving Sunday. We shook hands as we parted. I would not see him again before I left for home. He had been a friend and had helped me several times during my six months at NPU.

Leaving Xi'an

G oodbye Xi'an

My six months in China was rapidly coming to an end. The project management conference had ended three weeks before, in early October. Since my arrival in Beijing, I had traveled to Tianjin, Dalian, Hefei, Suzhou, Wuhan, traveled through the Three Gorges of the Yangtze River to Chongqing and finally to remote Guiyang before returning to Xi'an and NPU. Now I was leaving to travel by train to Tianjin, a trip that would take over 36 hours. There I would visit friends for a few days before flying home.

It was a cool overcast morning with the promise of rain. The air chilled as the temperature fell. My bags were packed. I was ready to go. Several friends came to my room to say goodbye. Those I remember are Zhou Li Ping and Wang Peng and Strawberry. Strawberry was a young Chinese woman with naturally red hair.

A university car was to pick me up at nine in the morning to drive me to the train station. The time to go had come. Leaving through the guest house front door I shook hands and said 'goodbye' to twenty or so friends who had come to see me off. This was a bittersweet moment. I was happy to be heading home but saddened to be leaving friends. Soon I would be half a world away.

The university car arrived, and we loaded my belongings into the trunk. Waving a last goodbye, I, Fupei and Sheng Wu, climbed into the car and off we went. Looking back, I had one last glimpse of my friends. The driver exited NPU via the South Gate and then drove across this ancient city to the train station. Soon the driver turned right and drove the entire length of the Ming wall that surrounds the oldest part of Xi'an. Construction on the wall began during the Tang dynasty, 618 to 907. Gradually expanded today the wall stands 40 feet tall, 40 to 46 feet across the top and 50 to 60 feet across the bottom. Surrounding the oldest part of the city it is 8.5 miles in length. I was glad to get one last long look.

Now I was off to home from halfway around the world. Would I ever see any of these friends or the city wall again? At that time, it seemed to me the odds were against my returning.

At the station, Fupei and Sheng Wu sat with me in the Soft Sleeper Customer Lounge. When the boarding call sounded at 2:20 p.m. they helped me with my suitcase to the car and compartment printed on my ticket. Entering the compartment, they put my suitcase on the wide shelf above the compartment door. I did not need help, but Chinese friends insist on helping; at times this makes things more difficult than is necessary. I placed my backpack on the foot end of the lower berth. Once settled I shook hands with both men. They left, returning to NPU. Rain was falling when the train began moving at 2:40 p.m. With melancholy I watched Xi'an roll past. The city thinned out and soon we were rolling through the countryside. The temperature continued to drop. I could feel cold radiating through the window. Thank goodness this was late enough in the year that it was permissible for the train to be heated.

I was in a soft sleeper compartment, where foreign travelers almost always travel. There was a sliding door with an inside lock. Four berths, two upper and two lower, made up the compartment. Between the lower berths, below the window, was a drop-leaf table, covered by a small tablecloth. Underneath the table stood two large thermos bottles filled with boiling water.

The hot water could be used by passengers for tea, coffee, or food, such as Ramen noodles. I could buy a variety of Ramen noodles from platform vendors at stops of five minutes or more. These quick cooking noodles came in a variety of flavors, from mild to very spicy. Four ceramic mugs sit on the table. Every three or four hours a train attendant refilled the thermoses. Fresh, clean bedding and a pillow lay on each berth. Attached to the wall beside each berth was a small, netted pocket to hold small personal items. This is where I put my glasses as I slept.

We rolled eastward through the tortured wind-swept Shaanxi landscape. Constant wind had eroded the loess soil land carving it into canyons, gullies and almost vertical-sided hills with flat tops and flat-bottomed valleys. This is the historic heartland of China from where Emperor Qin waged war and is credited with forming the first unified China. Shaanxi and Xi'an served as the capital for several thousand years.

Shaanxi natives say, "Beijingers are new Chinese. They have only been there a thousand years."

Bricks made of straw and mud are used to construct homes in peasant villages. My feeling was these houses must be very dark inside, especially during a gray rainy day. Walls surrounding the villages are constructed with the same materials.

Village streets were muddy, not paved and on this day, they were wet, cold, and slippery. I knew from experience that loess soil becomes slick when wet. It is like walking on ice. Olympic skaters could practice on it if it were firmer. Villagers walking flat footed on the slick mud. Their shoulders hunched forward. Their hands tucked inside pockets. No one carried an umbrella. No one wore a raincoat. Pigs and chickens went about doing what pigs and chickens do, seemingly impervious to the cold rain.

Occasionally I caught a glimpse of a cave home. These are not natural caves, but caves hand hewed into the hills by peasants. They are still in use in Shaanxi. Dug into the loess soil these homes are easy to heat in the winter and, like caves, stay cool in the summer. Inside stairways lead from one level to another. If I were a Shaanxi peasant, this is the type of dwelling that I would like to have as my home.

Korean Sisters

Soft sleeper compartments are always full and strangers, regardless of gender, travel together. Above me was a man, I took to be Chinese. On the other side were two young women. I assumed they were Chinese. Later they told me they were Korean sisters and had been studying Chinese in China. The man above never moved nor spoke the entire trip. I have no idea how he managed to not move in 36 hours.

The train continued East, past Hua Shan, one of the five sacred mountains in China and the most dangerous to climb. Friends at the university often said to me, "You should climb Hua Shan, people die there every year." People climb at night so they can be on the top as the sun rises. But the view from the top makes the effort worthwhile. Yes," I would think, "what is it you are really saying." However, I knew they meant well.

We crossed the Yellow River at last light. Darkness was deepening quickly. Looking out the window I saw the Yellow River, far below. The water looked more like flowing mud than water. I settled into my bunk for the night.

The route up to this point was the same as if I were going to Beijing. Later during the night this train, after passing through Taiyuan, the capital of Shanxi Provence, would continue to the East, passing north of Beijing and on to Tianjin.

When I looked up one of the young women pointing to me and then to herself asked, "You American?" Pointing to herself she continued, "English bad."

"Yes, I am American. My Korean is zero," I replied showing a zero with my hand.

The two laughed. "You speak Chinese?"

"Yi din-din, a little bit," I replied.

We began talking, mixing English and Chinese. Surprisingly with their little bit of English and my Yi din-din in Chinese we were able to have a good conversation. They were sisters studying Chinese at Tianjin Normal University, the same school I stayed at for several days. One was leaving for home soon. The second sister was staying another six months continuing her Chinese studies. She hoped to become a translator.

Soon I settled down for the night. The sisters talked in low voices, the wheels clicked on the rails and my thoughts turned to home, half a world away.

Before settling down to sleep one sister ask, "Are you a ....."? She paused, thinking and then made the sign of the cross.

"Yes," I said. "I am a Christian."

This pleased them. She replied pointing to her sister and herself. She made the sign of the cross, they were Catholic.

Morning

The next morning, we continued talking as the train rolled through Eastern China. The schedule was for us to arrive in Tianjin in the late afternoon. The flat, fallow, brown barren countryside was of little interest. We were too far north for rice. The fields, once filled with the yellow bloom of rapeseed were now brown and empty.

Arriving on schedule in Tianjin I helped the sisters take their luggage down from overhead. They left the train ahead of me. I then took my suitcase down, put on my backpack and slowly struggled to the exit at the end of the car. As I climbed off the train, I noticed they stood watching, making sure that I successfully got off the train. Later I saw them waiting and watching until they saw that my friend Li Zhi had met me. Obviously, they were going to help me if they saw I had a need. I thought this was nice of them.

Tianjin, my last stop before flying home, if I succeeded in having my visa extended all would be right with the world.

Tianjin ... Again

Goodbye to the dragon

Visa Extension

Once I explained my visa problem to Le Zhi, she agreed to go with me to the office of the Tianjin Security police. We met at 9 a.m. and took a bus to the police station. After we entered the building. a man directed us down a short hallway. At the end of the hallway, to our left, was a counter. A young woman sat in front of a typewriter. As we walked up, she smiled and spoke. Li explained my problem. After a short conversation, Li turned to me, "Let her have your passport."

I handed the passport to her. Deftly she opened it and flipped to the page showing my Chinese visa. She carefully checked it and then turned to a clean page. Whack went her rubber stamp. Picking up a fountain pen she entered the extension date. Smiling she handed the passport to me. With great relief, I took it and said a heart full "Xie, xie." [Thank you.]

"Bù kèqì" [don't be polite] she replied. Then she handed me a bill for ¥52.00, about $6.50.

Before leaving I had Li ask her what happens when a person appears at customs in the Beijing airport with an expired visa.

"Oh, they renew it and charge ¥500." That converted to about $62.50.

Now I was clear to fly home in five days. My flights would be from Beijing to Narita, Japan on Monday, October 30th. I was booked to spend one night at the Air Japan hotel and then to fly out of Japan on October 31st. Because of the International Date Line my landing at Dulles, after a twelve-hour flight would be twenty minutes before I took off ... at least by the clock.

Sent to the Country for Re-education

Li Zhi, her son, and I ate lunch at Brownie's. Li said, Brownie's is a Canadian based fast-food restaurant." We had planned on having Bouzi at a well-known Chinese restaurant, but it was so crowded, and service was so slow we changed our plans. Brownie's served chicken platters and sandwiches. Li and I opted for a sandwich each. Li's son, Han Biano, chose a chicken platter, two pieces of chicken, Cole slaw, mashed potatoes, and a roll.

After eating, we caught a taxi to the middle school where Li taught English. I do not remember what Han Biao did. Perhaps we dropped him off at his elementary school. While Li taught, I stayed in her office, talking to one of her coworkers, a man.

He said he was born in Tianjin. At age 16, during the Cultural Revolution, he was sent to the countryside. He was a member of what in China now called the Lost Generation. Thousands upon thousands of young people were pulled out of school, ripped away from their home to be sent to the countryside to work; it was called re-education. Most of that generation never had a chance of further education and no future other than working with the peasants or in factories.

After three years his assignment was to work in a factory. "I was depressed," he said. "There was no future, nothing to look forward to other than a hard life in poverty." While at the factory he began teaching himself English. Several years later he received permission to leave factory work and attend a university where he majored in English. Upon graduation, he taught English in the Provence of Hubei. He did not say at what level he taught. Finally, after four years of teaching, he received permission to return to Tianjin. Now he teaches English in a middle school. Married with a ten-year-old daughter, he said that life is much better. I sensed he wanted to tell me more, but there were other teachers within hearing. He was not the only person I talked to in China who seemed reluctant to talk openly when others were nearby.

Trip Home

Tianjin to Narita, Japan

The car reserved by Li Zhu arrived a few minutes after 10:00 a.m. I had checked out of the university guest house fifteen or twenty minutes earlier, walked outside, and waited at the curb. My bill, for seven days at the guest house, was 850.00 RMB or $105.00. I considered $15.00 a night a reasonable price. The bedroom and toilet were clean. There was a working TV, albeit there were no channels in English. That limited my interest in watching anything beyond movies at night. Dialogue is not necessary to have some understanding in action movies. I climbed into the car, and we were off. I was on my way home.

Los Angeles has nothing on traffic gridlock in Tianjin. An hour after leaving the university guest house, we finally passed from the city into the countryside. In the stop-and-go traffic of the city we were beside a large van for at least half an hour. This would not be memorable, but I noticed that all the windows were barred, and the van was filled with young men.

"That's strange," I mused, "the young men are secure inside the van, but it would be hard for them to get out if there was an emergency."

Li Zhi looked at the van. "Bad boys on their way to jail," she said. "They should have listened to their mother."

We chatted, wondering what the men had done and how long they would be in jail. I had the feeling that a Chinese jail was not the most pleasant place in which to live for any length of time.

Ten miles further she pointed to our right. "There is the prison where they are going. I do not believe they will like being there."

Once we were out of the city and onto the limited access highway that connects Tianjin and Beijing, the driver sped up. Glancing at the speedometer I saw that we were traveling at 140 kilometers an hour. This converts to 87 miles per hour. The trip to Beijing International Airport took two hours and twenty-five minutes. The car pulled to a stop in front of the terminal at 12:30 p.m. Li and I climbed out and entered the international arrivals and departures terminal. The driver left to park the car.

It isn't just Tianjin that has a traffic problem. My impression is that any medium to large city in China is plagued with traffic problems. To me, this seemed a contradiction. China was encouraging its citizens to buy cars and at the same time imposing draconian measures to cut down on traffic. During the world table tennis championship last spring, drivers could drive into the city only on odd or even days depending on the ending number on the license plate. For instance, a car with a license ending in 3 could drive only on odd-numbered days. A license ending in a 6 could only drive within the city on even-numbered days.

In October 1995 every vehicle entering Beijing not carrying a Beijing license tag had to stop at a roadside station some distance outside the city and show cause why they should be allowed to enter the city. If satisfied, the driver was given a permit to display on the front windshield. The limited-access highway was not busy this morning and our wait for the permit was short. I can't imagine the chaos this policy would create in Washington, D.C. Though this permit system may exist for other Chinese cities this was the only time I saw it in place or knew of its existence.

By this time the driver had parked and found us. Our plan was to have lunch together. Sadly, there was no restaurant in that area of the terminal. There was no reason to stay where we were, and Li Zhi could not go with me past customs. With a hug, we said our final goodbye. Li and the driver left. They were going to stop in Beijing for lunch before driving back to Tianjin.

Once I entered the terminal, I went to the desk to buy an exit permit. China, like various countries I have visited, has a departure tax. A traveler must have the departure tax receipt to clear customs and progress to the departure gate. In 1995 the cost of the departure tax was 90 RMB, about $12.00.

Stopping at the Japanese Airline counter I checked my suitcase through to Washington, Dulles. I was glad to see it disappear on its way to the airplane and glad that I would not see it again until I arrived at Dulles outside of Washington, D.C. There would be no struggle in Japan with this heavy item.

The agent wrote my seat assignment on the ticket envelope. Happily, I found that just like last spring I was seated just behind a large emergency door. I would have no worries about knee or leg room. There would be no bothering others whenever I left the seat for any reason. "Your departure gate is number 7," the agent said.

I have no memory of clearing customs or any security checks. If I had experienced any problem, I am sure I would remember and would have noted it in a final letter home. I handed the letter, number 123, and gave it to Nancy when we were home in Annapolis. This is the value of letters or a journal. Faint or bold ink will remind the writer years hence of events completely forgotten.

I made my way to Gate #7 where I would board the flight to Narita. There I would spend the night at the Hotel Narita Nikko just as I had on my trip to Beijing, and fly on to Washington, D.C. the next morning. It was now 2:00 p.m. The sign at the gate showed that boarding would begin at 2:35 p.m. Takeoff was scheduled for 3:05. However, we lifted off the ground 25 minutes late. Except for a bit of turbulence just off the Chinese coast, it was a smooth flight. There must have been a tailwind since we landed 15 minutes earlier than scheduled.

Because my suitcase was already checked through to my destination, I did not have to wait at the carousel. I walked past the carousel area and on to Japanese customs. It was a bit strange walking to the customs agent alone. No other traveler was in the room. I handed him my passport.

"Where is your suitcase?" he wanted to ask.

"I checked it through in Beijing to Washington, D.C. I have all I need in my backpack."

"What will you do while you are in Japan?"

" I am going to catch the bus to the JAL hotel. I'll spend the night there and fly on tomorrow."

He looked at me and then stamped my passport. "Have a good evening," he said and waved me through to the exit door.

Japan to the USA

I left customs and made my way to the bus stop to catch the JAL bus that would take me to their hotel, the Nikko Narita. I knew where to go as I had caught the same bus last spring and in 1992 when Nancy and I worked at NPU for a month. In about five minutes the bus pulled up. Like the English the Japanese drive on the' wrong' side of the road, the left side. Climbing aboard we were soon off.

I checked in. picked up my breakfast coupon and room key. As the desk clerk handed me my breakfast coupon and key to room #546 she said, "When you check out, you can pick up your boarding pass."

I was surprised and then realized that as the hotel belonged to the airline this made sense. The hotel computer was tied to the reservation computer. "That's great," I exclaimed. "That means I will not have to check in tomorrow morning at the terminal."

"Only if you have something to check onto the flight, such as a suitcase," she replied.

Smiling, I told her that I had checked my suitcase from Beijing to Washington, D.C.

"Then you can go directly through security and go straight to the gate."

This was good news; indeed, no hassle at a ticket counter and that would cut down the amount of time I needed to walk to the departure gate.

I rode the elevator to the 5th floor and walked to my room. It was small. That was fine. I only needed a bed and a bathroom. The bathroom was to my left and a step or two past the bathroom door, again to my left was the bed. There was a low bed wide shelf over the bed that gave the traveler storage space. It was much like getting into a bunk bed except there was no upper bunk. A step past the bed to the right was a single soft chair and a small table. To the left was a small writing space. Attached to the wall hung a television. The travels of the day left me feeling grimy and tired ... time for a shower. Hot water feels so good after a day of travel. A most luxurious, thick white bathrobe hung in the bathroom. Ah, it was so comfortable. I must admit it was a temptation to buy one, but I had nowhere to pack it ... that was probably a good thing.

Breakfast bar

Monday, October 30th, 1995- Flight Home

Always a morning person I awoke at 5:15 a.m. At 6:15, I made my way to the restaurant for their buffet breakfast. It was the same as last spring, a mixture of eastern and western food. I was not the first there as the restaurant was three-quarters filled. My flight did not leave until noon, I had plenty of time, so I enjoyed a leisurely breakfast. Ah, real orange juice, what a pleasure after six months with neither canned nor fresh orange juice, good coffee, good eggs, or good bacon.

I returned to my room, checked the pockets of my journalist jacket making sure I had all I needed packed in the right pockets. At 8:00 I walked to the lobby. Surprisingly there was no line at the reception desk. Walking to the desk, I picked up my boarding pass, seat 35K. The lady at the room registration desk suggested I catch the 10:30 bus. I thought for a minute and decided to catch the 10:00 bus. I always like a cushion of time to clear customs and go to the boarding gate. I do not like to rush. Waiting at the airport could not be as boring as sitting in a small, one-chaired room and is less stressful than correcting a problem when the time is short. I returned to my room.

I was in the lobby by 9:45 a.m. The 10:00 bus was sitting outside the front door. Leaving the lobby, I made my way to the bus. The driver motioned for me to climb aboard. Five or six others climbed aboard with me. I was relieved and relaxed to be on my way. A good night of sleep does wonders.

Soon the bus began to move, and we were on our way. There was little to see, but I watched intently gathering in as many sights as I could during the ten-minute ride to the airport checkpoint. The driver opened the door. Two customs agents climbed onboard. I handed one my passport. After a careful check, he handed it back to me. After checking each passenger, the agents were satisfied. Exiting the bus, they waved to the driver to go ahead to the terminal.

Japanese Customs is efficient, and I was cleared to go to the boarding gate. I was thirsty, so I stopped at a small shop and bought a cup of Coke, $2.50. Then I made my way to gate B-73. The Boeing 747 was being towed into place as I walked into the waiting area. It was 10:45, an hour and fifteen minutes before takeoff and only 45 minutes before boarding began. Leaving the hotel at 10:00 suddenly looked like a good decision. A flight attendant told me the flight on November 28th would be the last JAL flight between the two cities.

There were many empty seats on the flight today. If this was normal, then I was not surprised the flight was scheduled to be canceled.

We boarded and I settled in for the long flight. During the announcements, the stewardess added, "The flight will be 720 minutes in length." This was interesting. I had never heard of the flight time being made in minutes; hours and minutes, yes … but just in minutes? No, this was new. "Let's see," I mused, "there are 60 minutes in an hour. Ten hours or 60 times 10 equals 600 minutes. Two more hours or 60 time 2 equals 120 minutes. So, it will be a twelve-hour flight, assuming we are on schedule. I thought 12 hours would give me a lot of time to count ceiling panels, look at clouds, sleep or read.

During the flight, two movies were shown, *Miami Rhapsody* and *The Englishman Who Went Up the Hill but Came Down a Mountain*. I can remember nothing about either movie. I assume I watched them. Also, we were fed two meals and a snack.

It was 5:00 a.m. as we crossed Alaska. A flight attendant stopped at my seat to tell me that if I moved to the other side of the plane, I would see the Northern Lights. I thought they would flash, but they were like long strands of smoke. It appeared that we were at the same altitude as the Northern Lights.

The rest of the flight went smoothly. Landing at Dulles I noted that we had taken off from Narita at 2:35 p.m. on Monday, October 30th and that we landed at 2:15 p.m. on Monday, October 30th … 20 minutes before we took off. I did not feel younger.

The plane arrived ahead of schedule. When I exited customs Nancy had just walked up and had not had time to sit down. And, thus, my 1995 China adventure came to an end.

Endnotes

[I] Orange Man and his family were obviously from a minority group in China. I have unsuccessfully tried to discover the name of this group.

[ii] By Kallgan - Own work, CC BY-SA 3.0, https://commons.wikimedia.org/w/index.php?curid=322968

[iii] By Rolf Müller (User:Rolfmueller) - Own work, CC BY-SA 3.0, https://commons.wikimedia.org/w/index.php?curid=1596229

[iv] Edgar Snow was an American journalist. His most famous book *is Red Star Over China* recounting his travels with Mao and the Communists in 1936. The book was published in 1937.

[Vi] Shoving does not seem to be considered impolite but a necessity when getting on buses in China.

[vii] Kipling, Rudyard, poem, *Mandalay*

[viii] Construction of such buildings boomed over all of China, leading to a crisis that at the time of this writing in December 2023 threatens the entire banking system.

[ix] Quánshì is almost impossible to translate directly into English. The world implies power and influence, but there is more in the meaning than those two words.

[x] Dofu is the Chinese word for Tofu. Tofu is the Japanese word. Both mean bean curd.

[xi] Berberova, Nina, *The Ladies of St. Petersburg,* (New Directions Books, New York, 1995) p26.

[xii] Jin-Mei-La was an orange-flavored soft drink that I often had with restaurant meals.

[xiii] In Maoist[1] thought, a **capitalist roader** (simplified Chinese[2]: ◇◇◇; traditional Chinese[3]: ◇◇◇; pinyin[4]: *Zǒu zīpài*) or (simplified Chinese[5]: ◇◇◇◇◇◇◇◇◇◇;

---

1.   https://en.wikipedia.org/wiki/Maoist

2.   https://en.wikipedia.org/wiki/Simplified_Chinese_characters

3.   https://en.wikipedia.org/wiki/Traditional_Chinese_characters

traditional Chinese[6]: ◇◇◇◇◇◇◇◇◇◇◇; pinyin[7]: *Zǒu zīběn zhǔyì dàolù dídàng quánpài*) is a person or group who demonstrates a marked tendency to bow to pressure from bourgeois[8] forces and subsequently attempts to pull the Revolution in a capitalist[9] direction. https://en.wikipedia.org/wiki/Capitalist_roader

[xiv]   http://www.nytimes.com/1989/06/18/weekinreview/the-world-unleashing-the-dark-methods-of-the-cultural-revolution.html

[xv] **Comfort women** were women and girls forced into sexual slavery[10] by the Imperial Japanese Army[11] in occupied territories before and during World War II[12]. https://en.wikipedia.org/wiki/Comfort_women

[xvi] You may have noticed I mention **Butterfly Lovers** several times. In China it is a beautiful and very popular concerto and one of my favorite pieces of music.

[xvii] http://www.fisheries.noaa.gov/pr/species/fish/chinese-sturgeon.html

[xviii] http://www.bbc.com/news/world-asia-china-29201926

[xix] www.chinatravel.com[13]

[xx] Why was I going to such a remote part of China? At that time a young Chinese man, Sun Hai, lived with my wife and me while he attended St. John's College in Annapolis, Maryland. He was born and grew up in Guiyang, the capital of Guizhou province. I was on my way to visit his mom and dad. Both were now retired and had just moved into a new apartment.

[xxi] Eastern toilets are simply a hole in the floor. The sanitation or lack thereof in the train toilets was such that I had no desire to have a 'throne' to sit on.

---

4.   https://en.wikipedia.org/wiki/Pinyin

5.   https://en.wikipedia.org/wiki/Simplified_Chinese_characters

6.   https://en.wikipedia.org/wiki/Traditional_Chinese_characters

7.   https://en.wikipedia.org/wiki/Pinyin

8.   https://en.wikipedia.org/wiki/Bourgeoisie

9.   https://en.wikipedia.org/wiki/Capitalism

10.   https://en.wikipedia.org/wiki/Sexual_slavery

11.   https://en.wikipedia.org/wiki/Imperial_Japanese_Army

12.   https://en.wikipedia.org/wiki/World_War_II

13.   http://www.chinatravel.com

Don't miss out!

Visit the website below and you can sign up to receive emails whenever William Lively publishes a new book. There's no charge and no obligation.

https://books2read.com/r/B-A-XAFV-TRFUC

Connecting independent readers to independent writers.

Did you love *Living With the Dragon*? Then you should read *Stepping Stones: The Army Years, 1960-1962*[14] by William Lively!

15

We travel through life stepping from stone to stone. Always we hope that we will not slip into the water, the mud, or worse. There are people ahead and behind us, as we walk through our life. Some help, some hinder. Each decision we make is a step toward a new stone. Here in these pages are some of the stones I stepped on during my life while in the Army – 1960-1962. I do not attempt to discuss the major events of that era. Rather, I try to show what life in the Army was like for the average enlisted man.

---

14. https://books2read.com/u/3Rz6AL

15. https://books2read.com/u/3Rz6AL

Also by William Lively

Stepping Stones
Stepping Stones: The Army Years, 1960-1962
Living With the Dragon

About the Author

Bill grew up in Rockingham County, VA. He attended James Madison University earning a BS degree following two years in the Army. He worked four years as an elementary school librarian and twenty-six years as the technical librarian for Aeronautical Radio, Inc., ARINC. He earned a graduate certificate in Technical Information Systems from American University and a masters degree in Library and Information Science from the Catholic University of America. He and his wife, Nancy worked several times at the Northwestern Polytechnical University in Xi'an, China. Later they worked in Prague, Czech Republic and Moscos, Russia creating OPACs for seminary libraries.

www.ingramcontent.com/pod-product-compliance
Lightning Source LLC
Chambersburg PA
CBHW061432150726
47987CB00001B/184